A LEAGUE OF THEIR OWN

THE BOOK OF SPORTING TRIVIA

HarperCollins*Publishers*
1 London Bridge Street
London SE1 9GF

www.harpercollins.co.uk

First published by HarperCollins*Publishers* 2015

1 3 5 7 9 10 8 6 4 2

A catalogue record of this book is available from the British Library.

HB ISBN 978-0-00-814927-7
EB ISBN 978-0-00-816619-9

Printed and bound in Spain by Graficas Estella, Spain

Commissioning Editor: Barbara Lee
Executive Producers: Jim Pullin, David Taylor, Murray Boland and Danielle Lux

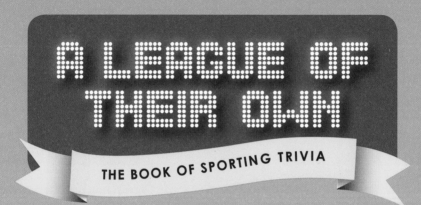

THE BOOK OF SPORTING TRIVIA

A LEAGUE OF THEIR OWN

THE BOOK OF SPORTING TRIVIA

For nine series now, some of the greatest sportsmen and women on the planet have joined James Corden, Jamie Redknapp, Freddie Flintoff and Jack Whitehall for all the fun and games on Sky 1's *A League of Their Own*. There's been F1 racing, rapping with John Barnes and, of course, the invention of the 'Mobot'.

We've learned a lot about our sports stars in that time: their likes, their dislikes, their hobbies, their fears, their preferred smells – even their favourite love songs.

Now, and for the very first time, we can present the fruit of those hundreds of hours of exhaustive and insightful research into what makes our sportsmen and women tick.

So whether you're at home, on the move or in a pedalo, sit back, relax and enjoy.

'This is really a
lovely horse.
I once rode her
mother.'

—

TED WALSH,
HORSE-RACING
COMMENTATOR

SUPERPOWER

Many fans believe their sports stars have superpowers, such are the mesmeric skills they produce under huge pressure. But if they could, what superpower would they possess?

GARETH BALE

The Welsh flyer has claimed his superpower would be flying. Cue no end of aerodynamic jokes thanks to a 2012 operation to have his ears pinned back when he was playing at Spurs.

WAYNE ROONEY

England rock Rooney, meanwhile, has revealed that he would like to see into the future. It's not a massive leap to predict that there will probably be more goals and less hair, Wayne.

CHRISTINE OHURUOGU

The former Olympic and world 400m champion wants to have the power of invisibility. She claimed, 'Being invisible would be fun.' She is rarely seen between major championships already.

ALTERNATIVE CAREER

Not many sports stars look back and wish they could have done something different. But, if they could, what kind of profession would they have chosen?

KEVIN PIETERSEN
The former England batsman revealed in a Twitter Q&A that he would have been a pilot.

WAYNE ROONEY
The United striker told the *Sun*, 'I always enjoyed RE, so I might have been a priest.'

JERMAIN DEFOE
The former Spurs, Portsmouth and England striker revealed, 'I think I'd have done something constructive because my mum, Sandra, was strict with me. I used to dance when I was young, street dancing. I've been on a float at Notting Hill Carnival!'

'They're the second-best team in the world, and there's no higher praise than that.'

Kevin Keegan

Here is Nicola Adams on a visit to Upton Park ...

... that's the only medal West Ham fans are likely to see

NICOLA ADAMS

BORN: 26 October 1982, Leeds, England
CAREER HIGHLIGHTS: Olympic gold, Commonwealth gold and three World silvers

1) Adams has blazed a trail for women's boxing in England since the age of 13. It took four years for her to find her second opponent, but when she did get regular quality opposition she wasted no time in lighting up the ring, including the English amateur title in 2003.

2) Silver at the 2007 European Amateurs represented the first time an English woman had medalled in a major tournament. She went one better at the London 2012 Olympics by becoming the first woman in history to claim a boxing gold medal with flyweight success.

3) Nicola tripped on the stairs in 2009 and was left in a brace for most of the following three months. Her 2012 Olympic dream was left in the balance, but she recovered full mobility and won funding to launch herself on the road to her famous gold in London.

4) Adams travelled to Brazil with David Cameron on a trade mission and visited the favelas where the British-run project Fight for Peace provides a haven for street kids. Sadly the prime minister didn't go 12 rounds in the ring as journalists queued in hope around the block.

DID YOU KNOW: Adams joined fellow Olympic medallists Dani King, Laura Trott, Beth Tweddle and Gemma Gibbons for a photoshoot where they dressed up as the Spice Girls. They should have given the singing a crack as it wouldn't be much worse than the original group.

BEST EVER

CRICKETERS' NICKNAMES

• Ashley Giles
'The King of Spain'

• Shane Warne
'Hollywood'

• Michael Holding
'Whispering Death'

• Lasith Malinga
'Malinga the Slinga'

• Monty Panesar
'The Python'

Harbhajan Singh
'The Turbanator'

Glenn McGrath
'Pigeon'

Ian Bell
'The Sherminator'

David Lloyd
'Bumble'

Stuart Broad
'Westlife'

Ian Botham
'Beefy'

HOW TO

BE A BRITISH TENNIS FAN

Not long ago, you could trundle into Wimbledon midway through the day and watch top tennis for the price of a cheap night out. These days, you need to queue for days and mortgage your house for an outside court. What makes a British tennis fan now? Find out below:

Only ever watch Wimbledon – and that's just for the 15 minutes it takes for every Brit except Murray to get knocked out.

Refer to all the top players by their first names even though they'd give you a powerful backhand into the face if you got near them.

Be one of the only people in Britain who sees a man wearing a tracksuit in a court and isn't reminded of their dad.

Realise that despite the fact you've only watched it on telly you're now Britain's number six.

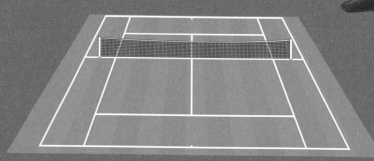

Laugh so hard
a bit of wee
comes out
because a
pigeon lands on
the court.

'We must have had 99 per cent of the game. It was the other 3 per cent that cost us the match.'

Ruud Gullit explaining a defeat

HOW TO

BE A PROFESSIONAL GOLFER

Check out our hit list of fairway essentials to look the part in plus fours:

Consider yourself an athlete although you play an estate agent's hobby for a living.

Dress like a cross between the Dorothy Perkins window display and a rodeo clown's nightmare looked at through a kaleidoscope.

During a 20-year career play like the world's greatest for the three days the Ryder Cup's on, then go back to being total dog crap the rest of the time.

Realise your main handicap is talking to members of the opposite sex.

Suspicions that Lance was cheating were first aroused
when he beat this guy in a race

LANCE ARMSTRONG

BORN: 18 September 1971, Plano, Texas, USA
CAREER HIGHLIGHTS: Doping to an extraordinarily brazen degree over many years

1) The Texan's cycling career was split into two stages, pre- and post-testicular cancer. Before his brush with death, Armstrong forged a highly impressive reputation as a big race rider in winning the 1993 World Championship and stages at the Grand Tour events in Europe.
2) Armstrong battled to overcome cancer and won the respect of many people around the world. Unfortunately for him and them, his entrance back into the sport coincided with rampant drug use that he spent years viciously denying in winning seven Tours de France.
3) He once admitted his confession was probably 'too late' – yes, not least because your confession came nearly three years after you'd been caught.
4) When asked if he got what he deserved, Armstrong said: 'I deserve to be punished. Not sure I deserve a death penalty.' To be fair, Lance, it'd be pretty hard to give you that as your tolerance to drugs is likely to be ridiculously high.

DID YOU KNOW: Armstrong dated singer Sheryl Crow from 2003 to 2006 – during which time she only released one new album, so maybe we shouldn't be so hard on him.

SPORTING SINGERS

Those of us unlucky enough to be around at the time of Hoddle and Waddle's 'Diamond Lights' know that sports stars and music do not mix. Here's a few other 'notable' efforts that have left poor fans reaching for their earplugs rather than their iTunes gift voucher.

CAROLINE WOZNIACKI

World number one tennis star Caroline Wozniacki released a heavily auto-tuned single called 'Oxygen' in 2012.

The stand-out moment is the lyric 'Boy, you're my match point', which was presumably written by someone who'd just received one of Caroline's 100mph serves to the head. Watching the video the song appears to be a 'love' story – in that zero people bought it.

We shouldn't be too critical, though, as Caroline did do it for charity – and I'm sure they were very grateful for the 3½ euros she raised.

BUBBA WATSON

Two-time Masters winning golfer Bubba Watson has released several songs, usually alongside fellow players Rickie Fowler, Ben Crane and Hunter Mahan. However, in 2014 he released a solo Christmas single under the name 'Bubba Claus', imaginatively titled 'The Single'.

The song's not a bad effort – even if Bubba does rhyme 'Dad' with 'Baghdad' but the video does let it down somewhat. I can't help thinking we'd all be able to guess what we were getting for Christmas if Santa's sack had 'PING' written on the side and a set of woods poking out the top.

NEW ORDER AND THE 1990 ENGLAND WORLD CUP SQUAD

Often considered the best ever football song, New Order's 'World in Motion' for Italia '90 reached number one that summer.

Everybody remembers John Barnes's rap – partly because we were shocked they didn't choose a more obvious candidate to perform it like Peter Beardsley or Dave Beasant.

In 1992 a group of wrestlers including 'legends' like 'Hacksaw' Jim Duggan, 'The Undertaker', Brett 'Hitman' Hart and 'Macho Man' Randy Savage released a record entitled *Wrestlemania: The Album*.

With songwriting duties taken on by Pete Waterman and the executive producing credit going to Simon Cowell you won't be surprised to hear it was a bit dross.

However, the single 'Slam Jam' proved a hit and stayed in the top ten for five weeks and reached number four – even if it did sound more like number two.

Tottenham Hotspur's regular musical collaborators Chas and Dave teamed up with a gang of snooker players under the name 'The Matchroom Mob' in 1986 to release 'Snooker Loopy'.

The brilliant lyrics include 'Now old Willy Thorne, his hair's all gone', which only works as a rhyme when sung in a cockney accent.

Sadly the boys haven't returned to the studio because any follow-up would surely be more hotly anticipated than the Stone Roses with *The Second Coming*.

HOW TO

BE A FOOTBALL SUPPORTER

Here's a step-by-step guide to surviving the ups and downs:

Declare your undying love for a team that actually make you unhappier than your wife leaving you or your nan dying.

Slate your team constantly – until someone else does. Then fight them.

Go to an away match and ridicule the other team's fans because it's not a sell-out, whilst refusing to notice that they sold out easily when Arsenal played there, so it's your team that's considered crap.

Get upset that the players don't interact with the fans – and send them death threats on Twitter because of it.

Hurl abuse at a player until he transfers – then complain that your team should never have sold him.

Go bare-chested in January so your fat man-breasts look like Smurfs' noses.

State confidently what you would've done in the World Cup final because you once had a game of Three and In at break-time at school.

Here he is ...

... at Royal Ascot on Ladies' Day

MARIO BALOTELLI

BORN: 12 August 1990, Palermo, Italy
PLAYER: Lumezzane, Inter Milan, Manchester City, AC Milan, Liverpool and Italy

1) Arguably the most enigmatic player of his generation, Balotelli made his first-team début for Lumezzane at the tender age of 15 in a Serie C1 match in 2006. Inter soon came sniffing around and he made his senior bow in December 2007, scoring two goals in his next game.
2) Balotelli scored 20 goals in 59 games ahead of his first cap for Italy in a friendly against the Ivory Coast and before his multi-million pound move to Manchester City. He helped them win the FA Cup in his first season, their first trophy in 35 years, and the Premier League title the next.
3) At Euro 2012, Balotelli said he refused to celebrate goals 'because I'm only doing my job. When a postman delivers letters, does he celebrate?' Given most companies say they'll deliver between 7am and Christmas, it's us who do somersaults if parcels arrive when we're in.
4) Balotelli's secret lover Chloe Evans once revealed, 'Being with him was like being in a circus. Imagine a cross between Willy Wonka, Michael Jackson and Peter Pan – and you've got Mario Balotelli.' If ever a comparison was a cue to cut short a relationship that was it.

DID YOU KNOW: Mario was asked by his mum to buy an ironing board for his cleaner. He came back five hours later with a lorry containing a quad bike, Scalextric and trampoline. Yacht salesmen were rubbing their hands in glee after he was sent out to buy curry soon after.

BEST FOOTBALLER LEGS

When you're poncing around on a pitch all week, there's a good chance footballers will have an attractive set of pins to show for it. Which player has the best legs according to Gaydar?

3. Frank Lampard

2. Theo Walcott

1.Steven
Gerrard

Here's Boris doing his best Jamie Redknapp impression

BORIS BECKER

BORN: 22 November 1967, Leimen, West Germany
CAREER HIGHLIGHTS: Six-time Grand Slam champion and two-time Davis Cup winner

1) Boris Becker catapulted himself, quite literally, into tennis fans' hearts by diving around the court en route to becoming the youngest ever winner of Wimbledon in 1985. Aged just 17, he also became the first German and the first unseeded champion in defeating Kevin Curren.

2) 'Der Bomber' proceeded to use his fierce serve to mop up a further five Grand Slam titles at Wimbledon, the Australian Open and US Open, but he never got past the semi-final stage at the French Open. He also won the Davis Cup twice and Olympic gold in doubles.

3) The German has claimed that he would like Steve McQueen to play him in the film of his life. Great idea, Boris, except for the fact that McQueen died in 1980.

4) Becker had a cheeky quickie with model Angela Ermakova on some stairs at London's Nobu restaurant in 1999, which resulted in her having his child. Bizarrely, it happened after an argument Boris had with his pregnant wife Barbara who thought she was in labour.

DID YOU KNOW: Boris has his own hair and body wash that 'is a commitment to style, sporty-elegant charisma and irresistible masculine effect'. Whether it entices attractive young women into romping with you in awkwardly small public places has yet to be ratified.

BUCKET LISTS

Sportsmen and women often achieve everything they ever want by reaching the top.
However, what do some want above all else before they pop their clogs?

LEWIS HAMILTON

The Formula 1 maverick doesn't exactly live a quiet life outside of the cockpit. Whether it's his high-profile celebrity relationship with ex-girlfriend Nicole Scherzinger or laying down tracks with the cream of the hip-hop crop, Lewis lives the dream. The two-time world champ, though, is still keen to take on the Mack Daddy of mountains – Mount Everest. In 2013 Lewis climbed Borneo's Mount Kinabalu, with his eyes now set on the highest in the world. The millionaire Mercedes man revealed, 'I plan to climb a lot of mountains over the next five to ten years, and eventually the big one at the end.'

DENNIS RODMAN

'The Worm' led the majority of his basketball career in the harsh glare of the spotlight, his zany antics giving tabloid editors continual big smiles outside of his ferocious defensive game for the likes of the Detroit Pistons and Chicago Bulls. Having done pretty much every outrageous thing ever known to mere mortals, Rodman revealed that he'd like to feel the wind through his hair in an entirely different way than normal for his bucket-list entry. The New Jersey boy said, 'I want to skydive Manhattan on Fifth Avenue, butt naked.'

JAMIE CARRAGHER

Liverpool's defensive rock for many years, Carra has gone on to grace the Sky pundit panel since his retirement. Never one to mince his words when pitted against former United rival Gary Neville, Carragher revealed an altogether bizarre wish. When asked on Twitter 'Have you ever put a cow through a mincer?' he replied, 'Not yet, but it's on the bucket list'!

Here's Usain with William and Kate.

Prince William's just saying, 'Sorry about Grandad –
he's from a different generation.'

USAIN BOLT

BORN: August 1986, Trelawny, Jamaica
CAREER HIGHLIGHTS: Six Olympic golds, eleven World golds and one Commonwealth gold

1) Bolt was sport mad growing up in Jamaica, alternating his time between athletics and football. He burst onto the international scene by winning the 200m at the 2002 World Juniors. It took him until 2007, though, to win his first senior medal with two World silvers.
2) The lanky Jamaican hit his sprinting stride fully by the 2008 Beijing Olympics, winning gold in the 100m, 200m and 4 x 100m relay. He repeated the feat in London four years later, racking up several more golds and world records at the World Championships in between.
3) Lightning Bolt found Chinese food 'odd' at the Beijing Olympics, so much so that he put his world record win down to a diet of McDonald's Chicken Nuggets. The Great Britain sprint team is now dining exclusively at Chicken Cottage ahead of the 2016 Rio Olympics.
4) The multiple world-record holder loves to party and one of his favourite haunts is the Oktoberfest in Munich. His favourite drink is an incredibly swift half.

DID YOU KNOW: Bolt pleaded with Villa fan Prince William to let son George grow up as a Manchester United supporter. He said, 'It isn't fair to put a child through that – especially not a prince.' Based on some of Charles N'Zogbia's crosses, baby George could do a job on the wing now.

BEST EVER

FOOTBALL CHANTS #1

One of the birthrights of any self-respecting football fan is the freedom to dream up hilarious or often nonsensical chants that hammer or big up players, managers and teams. A match isn't quite complete without a raucous group of fans bellowing out gems such as these:

'There's only one Emile Heskey, one Emile Heskey. He used to be sh**e, but now he's all right, Walking in a Heskey wonderland.'
Sung to the tune of 'Winter Wonderland' by Birmingham City fans after Emile Heskey's implausible return to form.

'He's here, he's there, he wears no underwear, Lee Bowyer, Lee Bowyer.'
This was sung by Leeds United fans after the player admitted he sometimes went commando.

'Don't blame it on the Biscan, Don't blame it on the Hamann, Don't blame it on the Finnan, Blame it on Traore. He just can't, he just can't, he just can't control his feet.'
Sung by Liverpool fans to the tune of 'Blame it on the Boogie' by The Jacksons, after Djimi 'Wobbly Legs' Traoré scored an own goal against Burnley in the FA Cup.

'When you're sat in row Z, and the ball hits your head, that's Zamora, that's Zamora.'
Sung to the tune of Dean Martin's 'That's Amoré', Fulham fans really knew how to show their appreciation for striker Bobby Zamora.

It was definitely sexier when Daniel Craig did it

IAN BOTHAM

BORN: 24 November 1955, Oldfield, England
PLAYER: Somerset, Queensland, Worcestershire, Durham and England

1) Despite having an offer to play football for Crystal Palace, Botham had his sights set on a career with his beloved Somerset and made his début in 1974. He famously took an Andy Roberts bouncer in his mouth, spat out some teeth and carried on his maverick batting.
2) His Somerset years alongside West Indian pals Viv Richards and Joel Garner harvested five trophies, while he also found time to play football for Yeovil Town and Scunthorpe United. As for England, he demolished bowlers and batsmen alike from 1977 to 1992.
3) Botham has been a long-standing charity fundraiser. He rafted down the Rhône and crossed the Alps with a troop of elephants in his widely publicised 1988 Hannibal Walk. He also allegedly unfurled a trunk of his very own in a controversial Twitter image during 2014.
4) 'Beefy' and Aussie Ian Chappell have an infamous feud dating back 36 years. The pair once nearly came to blows in a car park after Chappell muttered an obscenity to his English nemesis. Botham apparently said, 'Just ******* wait till I get him on my own in a lift.'

DID YOU KNOW: In 1985 a Hollywood director touted Botham as the next James Bond. They asked him to live in California for six months and hang out with the likes of Rod Stewart. Botham, however, didn't want to miss an important three-dayer at Scarborough.

SPORTING ACTORS

The bright lights of Hollywood aren't too far from the glare of the stadium spotlights. We take a look at a couple that dabbled in the acting game along with a few who have arguably forged bigger reputations on screen than they ever did in the arena.

Vinnie is one of the most successful sportsmen turned actors as he's appeared in over 70 films, including his electrifying début in *Lock, Stock and Two Smoking Barrels*.

He has a wide acting range whether he is playing a very hard bloke from London in *Snatch*, a very hard bloke from London in *X-Men: The Last Stand*, or a very hard bloke from London in *Madagascar 3: Europe's Most Wanted*.

Former world heavyweight champion Mike Tyson has appeared in 12 films, including *The Hangover* and *Entourage*.

It's unclear if he was actually cast in any of the films or if no one had the guts to tell a convicted criminal boxing champion that they didn't want him.

The people who had the easiest ride with Tyson on set were the caterers, who only had to provide food that was nicer than Evander Holyfield's ear.

ARNOLD SCHWARZENEGGER

Arnie's world famous for his appearances in movies like the *Terminator* films, *Total Recall* and *The Expendables*, but you may not realise that he started out as a champion bodybuilder.

Interestingly, Arnie was overdubbed in his early films. So although low-budget film-makers didn't think he sounded good enough for their straight-to-video dross, the people of California thought he sounded good enough to be in charge of the world's sixth largest economy.

MICHAEL JORDAN

The world's greatest ever basketball player made a big-screen appearance in Bugs Bunny film *Space Jam*.

Michael's performance was very impressive as despite acting alongside cartoon characters Daffy Duck and Porky Pig he was still the most one dimensional.

DWAYNE 'THE ROCK' JOHNSON

Former wrestler 'The Rock' has carved out a great career as an action star in films like *The Mummy Returns* and *The Fast and Furious* series.

However, I can't help thinking that the 6ft 5in muscle man may've been badly cast in the upcoming biopic of Warwick Davis.

DID YOU KNOW: The Frenchman went into acting after he retired, but his most famous role was playing himself in Ken Loach's *Looking for Eric*. The F-word is used around 200 times in the film – just less than Simmons used it after getting that karate kick.

And here he is playing the lead role in a new film called *Neil Ruddock: The Movie*

ERIC CANTONA

BORN: 24 May 1966, Marseille, France
PLAYER: Auxerre, Marseille, Montpellier, Nîmes, Leeds United, Manchester United and France

1) Even from an early age, Cantona managed to mix on-field genius with a combustible personality that often saw him fall foul of the football authorities. He made a name for himself as a forward at Auxerre as well as a handy fighter after decking a team-mate.
2) His electric performances for the French club and the national side, including a hat-trick against England at the 1988 U21 European Championships, saw his boyhood club Marseille pay a French record fee for his services. Sadly, the move and his career in France stalled.
3) After Sheffield Wednesday boss Trevor Francis turned down the chance to sign him, most probably after seeing his disciplinary rap sheet from France, Leeds stepped in and he helped them win the title before going on to become a Manchester United legend for five years.
4) His infamous kung-fu kick on Palace fan Matthew Simmons saw him banned and fined, but in 2011 Cantona admitted it was 'a great feeling' and a memory for fans to treasure. So, why not get Simmons's nipple from Eric's studs and put it in the national football museum?

DOWNTIME

When you add up the hours spent actually competing, sports stars only spend a fraction of their week in combat. How do they chill out, then, in between the occasional training session?

GLEN JOHNSON

Liverpool right-back Johnson is not like your stereotypical footballer when it comes to chilling out between training and games. Instead of spending hours glued to the screen playing video games, he studied for a maths degree. The England star spends two hours a day poring over Open University algebra and trigonometry, and often gets his team-mates to test him on coach journeys to matches. The former Portsmouth player explained, 'I've always liked maths so I thought, "Why not? There's not a job in the world that maths can't help you with." My teachers used to say, "You ain't going to achieve anything." The last thing they'd expect me to do is a maths degree. But anyone can do anything if they put their mind to it.'

$$2 + 2 = 5x$$

JAN VERTONGHEN

Tottenham's defensive lynchpin is a dab hand at pub quizzes and liked nothing better than to hit the boozer each week in Amsterdam for a thorough brain workout during his trophy-fuelled Ajax days. The Belgian international revealed, 'I love to do it because I can't really go out. It's my version of going out. I don't go to drink beer. My best subject is sport, but I think I also know something about the world. I haven't found a pub in England which does a good quiz yet. At the moment, I think the questions might be too English-based for me.'

PEP GUARDIOLA

The Bayern Munich manager is not your conventional top-flight boss. Former Spanish international Guardiola is a keen poet in his time away from the goldfish bowl of managing the Bundesliga giants and often recites his poems in public. Pep plucked up the courage to recite one at a charity event alongside singer Lluís Llach. One such line from the poem 'Life Is a Journey' reads like this: 'I hold a stone in my hands and every night I let it fall into the deep well of the sun and I take it out the next day, soaked in life.' Cantona would be proud.

Here's a shot of Andy as Liverpool fans will remember him best

ANDY CARROLL

BORN: 6 January 1989, Gateshead, England
PLAYER: Newcastle United, Liverpool, West Ham and England

1) Carroll became the youngest ever player to represent Newcastle United in Europe aged 17 years and 300 days when he replaced cult Peruvian Nobby Solano in a 1–0 win over Palermo in November 2006. He made his Premier League début against Wigan in February 2007.

2) The giant striker soon made a name for himself on Tyneside by banging in the goals with his noggin and left peg. After racking up 31 goals in 80 games, Liverpool came calling with a humungous £35 million bid that the Magpies snapped up in the January 2011 transfer window.

3) In January 2015 Carroll's fiancée posted several pictures of their house, dubbed 'Carroll Castle', on social media. In a blatant bid to upstage fellow WAGS, she has installed mirrored ceilings, zebra-print walls, a fuchsia sofa and a fully functioning beauty parlour.

4) Avatar (the nickname given to him after his blockbusting Newcastle displays) claimed to have once held the headstand position for six minutes and 31 seconds after a Dubai yoga session. He posted a photo as evidence. Copycat attempts have been few and far between.

DID YOU KNOW: Carroll once showed off his DIY skills by uploading a picture of himself assembling a rocking chair. Given the poor feller's injury record, we're surprised it wasn't a wheelchair.

BANNED WHAT?

Managers have various ways of getting their players in line if they are new to the club or if the squad's gone south. Here's a few of the best we've collared from the dugout archives:

DAVID MOYES

Real Sociedad boss Moyes did not cover himself in glory during his brief reign at Manchester United trying to fill the gigantic boots of Sir Alex Ferguson. Not content with presiding over several woeful defeats, Moyes also cancelled the traditional Christmas pantomime, performed by the United youth players, in favour of a manager's speech. Fergie used to serve soup wearing a pinny before settling down to watch the panto, with one cheeky youngster in 2010 appearing as Shrek with a curly wig to mock Wayne Rooney's hair transplant.

FABIO CAPELLO

The Italian built up an enviable CV at the likes of AC Milan, Real Madrid, Roma and Juventus before he hopped over the Channel to England to try and revive the national team. Sadly, he lost a fair few England players straight off the bat in the first training session by banning hotel visitors, WAGS, mobile phones and flip-flops. Not content with those bans, strict disciplinarian Capello also stopped the use of player nicknames – an English birthright.

ALAN PARDEW

'Pards' has never been shy of taking an unpopular decision at the helm of his various clubs to try and raise a sinking ship from the depths of despair. When he was manager at Charlton, Pardew even banned promising youngster Jonjo Shelvey from dancing at his school prom. He told Shelvey, who has since gone on to represent England, 'Just tell that girl and the teachers that you will not be dancing at the school prom.' Pardew also called off the Christmas party up at Newcastle when the Magpies trotted out a string of dismal winter performances. He declared, 'It's out of respect to our fans and what we have served them this year. There's no party for us, and the same for the staff. That's how it should be.'

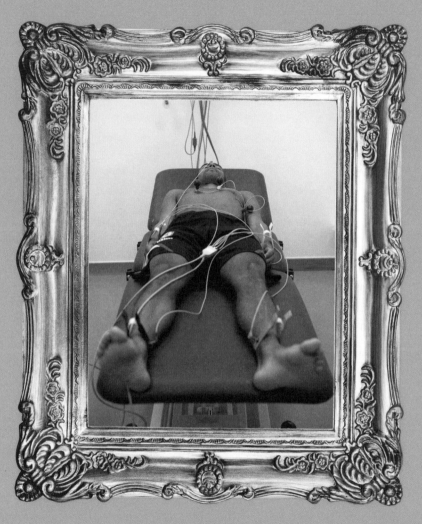

Here's Ashley – exhausted after trying to install BT Sport

ASHLEY COLE

BORN: 20 December 1980, Stepney, London, England
PLAYER: Arsenal, Crystal Palace, Chelsea, Roma and England

1) The England veteran started his career as a teenager by joining his local club, Arsenal, whom he had supported as a child. He signed as a professional on 25 February 2000 and quickly made a name for himself as a left-back on loan across London at Crystal Palace.
2) One of Arsène Wenger's 2003–04 season 'Invincibles', he made over 150 appearances for the Gunners and locked down the England left-back spot before undertaking a highly controversial switch to title rivals Chelsea after going behind the north London club's back.
3) Cole accidentally shot student Tom Cowan who was on work experience at Chelsea's Cobham training ground in 2011. He claimed he was unaware the .22 calibre air rifle was loaded and apologised to Cowan, who now flinches every time he hears a car backfire.
4) He also has the dubious honour of being named the most hated man in Britain in a website vote by 3,000 women. Fellow footballing love rat John Terry came in second, with crazy cleric Abu Hamza third, whose hook hand never seems to go down well with the ladies.

DID YOU KNOW: Ashley was once spotted on holiday spending £20,000 on bottles of champagne for himself and his friends. I'm not sure who was most shocked – Ashley's friends or the staff in the Wetherspoon's blowing the dust off the champagne.

BEST EVER

FOOTBALL CHANTS #2

'His name is Rio and he watches from the stand.'
Manchester United's Rio Ferdinand faced this chant after he was banned for missing a drugs test in 2003, sung to the tune of 'Rio' by Duran Duran.

'You should have stayed on the telly.'
Alan Shearer suffered this chant when he stopped working on *Match of the Day* to take charge of Newcastle United, but wasn't able to save them from being relegated.

'He's fast, he's red, he talks like Father Ted, Robbie Keane.'
Liverpool fans' salute to their striker.

'Your teeth are offside, your teeth are offside, Luis Suárez, your teeth are offside.'
Manchester United fans singing about Liverpool forward Luis Suárez's large gnashers.

'Deep fry yer pizzas, we're gonna deep fry yer pizzas.'
Scotland fans made this threat against Italy's cuisine in a World Cup qualifier in March 2007.

'Chelsea, wherever you may be, keep your wife from John Terry.'
Sung to the tune of 'Lord of the Dance', Chelsea fans saluted their captain after his alleged affairs.

'John Carew, Carew. He likes a lap-dance or two. He might even pay for you. John Carew, Carew.'
Sung to the tune of 'Que Sera, Sera' by Doris Day, this was the Villa fans' tribute to their player after he was caught visiting a gentlemen's club in 2008.

'You only live round the corner.'
Fulham fans to Manchester United supporters during their 2–0 win in the 2008/09 season.

'He's bald, He's red, He sleeps in Fergie's bed! Howard Webb, Howard Webb!'
Liverpool fans against Howard Webb and Manchester United manager Alex Ferguson.

'He's coming for you, He's coming for youuuuu, Harry Potter, He's coming for you.'
West Ham fans to Liverpool's Jonjo Shelvey given his resemblance to Lord Voldemort.

HOW TO

BE A TOP SNOOKER PLAYER

Here's the check list to ace it as a player:

Spend your youth in pubs, then either die of alcoholism or get really good at snooker.

Buy your 'sportswear' from the same shop waiters get their clothes.

Clear the table far more quickly at dinnertime than in any match.

Always stifle your giggles when you 'pot the pink'.

Give yourself a nickname like 'The Destroyer' even though your best ever game took seven hours and was only watched by a woman who was knitting.

"

'There is no in between – you're either good or bad. We were in between.'

—

Gary Lineker

"

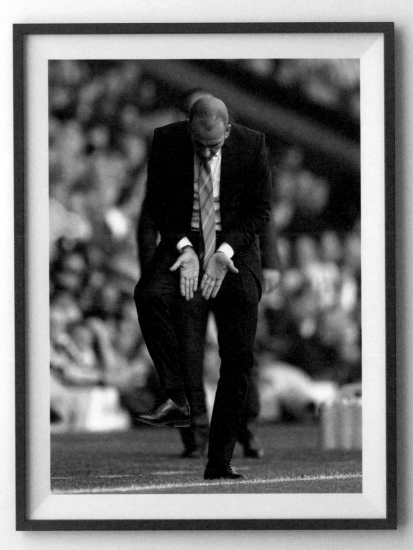

Here's Paolo starting an argument with his own shoe

PAOLO DI CANIO

BORN: 9 July 1968, Rome, Italy
PLAYER: Lazio, Juventus, Napoli, AC Milan, Celtic, Sheffield Wednesday and West Ham
MANAGER: Swindon Town and Sunderland

1) One of football's most bonkers characters, Di Canio started out at Lazio where he achieved cult status after scoring in the Rome derby to help the club escape relegation from Serie A. Rows with Giovanni Trapattoni at Juve and Fabio Capello at AC Milan saw him join Celtic.

2) He won SFA Player of the Year in his only season north of the border before heading south to Sheffield Wednesday where he continued to bang in the goals. He also shoved over referee Paul Alcock in a famous incident that earned him a £10,000 fine and an 11-game ban.

3) When Swindon were under a transfer embargo in January 2013, the Italian manager offered to pay £30,000 of his own money to keep loan players John Bostock, Chris Martin and Danny Hollands at the club. Many fans would have paid that to see him leave the club.

4) Paolo expressed admiration for dictator Benito Mussolini in his autobiography. Di Canio held fellow Italian Mussolini up as 'basically a very principled, ethical individual' who was 'deeply misunderstood'. So, was the Fascism, violence and alliance with Hitler a prank?

DID YOU KNOW: In his peculiar spell as Sunderland boss, Di Canio demanded that the Premier League side's foreign stars must learn five new words in English each day or face a hefty fine. The English players were soon found looking nervous in the canteen at the news.

FAVOURITE LOVE SONG

Everyone loves a mushy love song and sports stars are no different. So which romantic ditties get them booked on the love train?

LEBRON JAMES

The basketball behemoth has dominated the hardcourt in the NBA and around the world for several years now, picking up titles, gold medals and widespread adulation along the way. When he's getting in the mood with high-school sweetheart Savannah, he has revealed that Usher's 'My Way' does the trick. The former Miami Heat forward also included Usher in his favourite iTunes playlist along with Eminem, Jay Z, Michael Jackson and rap legend Nas.

MARIA SHARAPOVA

Russia's darling has had a string of celebrity boyfriends including Maroon 5 singer Adam Levine, basketball player Sasha Vujačić and fellow tennis player Grigor Dimitrov. When she's not winning the grand slams perennial nemesis Serena Williams gifts to her, she has revealed that she likes to board the jiggy train with Damien Rice's 'The Blower's Daughter' playing in her ears. She said, 'O is one of my favourite albums and this song is one of those sad love songs that you can listen to even when everything is OK with your love life.' No word as of yet whether Maria prefers this as a prelude to the main act or the act itself.

EVANDER HOLYFIELD

American Holyfield has enjoyed a quite spectacular career in the ring, defeating the likes of heavyweight legends George Foreman, Larry Holmes, Riddick Bowe and Mike Tyson along the way. 'The Real Deal' has also been quite the hit with the ladies. Not content with your classic two point four family life, the Alabama charmer has sired eleven children with six different women. When he's firing up the love machine, Holyfield has revealed that Barry White's 'Just the Way You Are' gets the vote for him. He declared, 'I grew up in the ghetto, the projects. Just because I was a poor person, people decided right then and there that they didn't want to get a chance to know me. So when I heard this song I wanted someone to like me just the way I was. I wanted to be loved for being me, opposed to being labelled and judged as someone who lived in the projects with all the stereotypes that go with it.'

Just after this photo, she whispered, 'No Sven, not here.'

SVEN-GÖRAN ERIKSSON

BORN: 5 February 1948, Sunne, Sweden
MANAGER: Gothenburg, Benfica, Roma, Sampdoria, Lazio,
England and Manchester City

1) Sven has one of the most interesting managerial CVs in football
after stopping off at several clubs around the world, usually for the
highest bidder. An average playing career finished in 1975, his first
two managerial gigs resulting in the UEFA Cup at Gothenburg.
2) Benfica came next and he enjoyed two excellent spells at the
Stadium of Light before filling the trophy cabinet at Lazio. Sadly for
England and Man City fans, he couldn't translate his magic touch
to either side, with two derby wins in one season over United a rare
highlight.
3) Jamie Carragher once described Sven as more of a playboy than a
manager. He said, 'The worse his status became as a football coach,
the better he became as a Casanova.'
4) In true Eriksson style, Sven rejected claims that his mammoth
£2 million a year wage package was excessive when he took over as
Ivory Coast manager. He declared, 'I'm not paid that well, but I'm
happy,' while reclining naked on a bed covered liberally with $100 bills.

DID YOU KNOW: Sven has a CD called *The Sven-Göran Eriksson
Classical Collection* including Hugo Alfven's 'Dance of the Shepherd
Girl' and Hubert Parry's 'Jerusalem'. Right Said Fred's 'I'm Too
Sexy' and Rod Stewart's 'Da Ya Think I'm Sexy?' are bonus tracks.

'I'M GOING TO MAKE A PREDICTION – IT COULD GO EITHER WAY.'

RON ATKINSON

BEST EVER

CRIME-STOPPERS

There's nothing quite like the heady tabloid mix of sports stars harnessing their inner Batman to foil crims up to no good. Who needs the police when you've got this lot out there protecting us?

KEN DOHERTY

Irish snooker star Ken Doherty was credited with stopping crime in his home city of Dublin. During his World Championship Final in 1997 against Stephen Hendry so many people were watching on RTE that not a single phone call was made to the police.

The police were so surprised they even contacted the telephone company to see if there was something wrong with the system.

JAVIER HERNÁNDEZ

Police in Mexico City have reported that there's a drop in the number of carjackings, muggings and robberies whenever Javier Hernández plays football.

Unfortunately fans tend to celebrate the goals he scores by gunning down members of rival drug gangs.

MANNY PACQUIAO

Ten times world boxing champion and the only man to win titles in eight different weight divisions, Manny Pacquiao is credited with actually stopping a war.

The army and guerrillas in his native Philippines stopped shooting at each other to celebrate his victory against Ricky Hatton.

If Manny can stop a war by beating Ricky Hatton then just think what they'd have been like if he'd defeated someone good!

HOW TO

BE AN NBA BASKETBALL PLAYER

Basketball is a global game now, from giant Chinese centres to tricky South Americans flinging passes around the court. Americans and the showbiz NBA still boss the hardcourt, of course, but whatever nationality you are, here's some easy steps to making it big in the footsteps of Magic, Jordan and co:

Remember your kit – or else you'll have to do it in your vest and pants.

Wear jewellery so large and sparkly it would be more appropriate to be hanging from the ceiling of an upmarket hotel.

Earn a college degree even though you only played basketball and did finger painting for four years.

Slam dunk and dangle off the ring like you're a hero – as if it doesn't happen 100 times in a game.

Get paid $20 million to wear shoes a Chinese child makes for 30p a month.

Here he is, regretting asking the hairdresser for a 'seventies minge'

LEWIS HAMILTON

BORN: 7 January 1985, Stevenage, England
CAREER HIGHLIGHTS: Two-time Formula 1 champion + GP2 and
Formula 3 champion

1) Hamilton was destined for greatness on the track from an early
age, the precocious racer dominating the karting circuit leading to an
invitation from McLaren head honcho Ron Dennis in 1998 to be part
of their driver development programme. Hamilton didn't look back.
2) After obliterating his rivals in Formula Three and GP2, Hamilton
eventually made his F1 début at the 2007 Australian GP. His maiden
victory arrived at the 2007 Canadian GP, with his first world title
earned on the final corner of the last race in the 2008 season in Brazil.
3) Lewis's father Anthony once wrote a letter to Tony Blair asking him
to save his son's F1 dream after he was excluded from school lessons
for allegedly kicking a fellow pupil. Sadly Blair was too busy building a
huge property empire at the taxpayer's expense to reply.
4) Roman Catholic Hamilton met with Pope Francis in 2014
during a Valentine weekend in Rome with ex Nicole Scherzinger.
He also posted an Instagram picture of them in the Sistine Chapel
captioned #godisthegreatest. #rosbergisthegreatest predictably
didn't make the cut.

DID YOU KNOW: Lewis claims he is a good sleeper and that the only
thing that prevents him is light. He said, 'I do not like it when the
room light's on.' Lewis might be shocked to hear, then, that the earth
is actually round and Bernie Ecclestone is only in F1 for the money.

FAVOURITE SMELL

Eau de Baby Smell

Sport relies on a few senses that when combined can rocket you to the top of your respective game. They rarely use smell, however, so what tickles the nose hairs of these top stars?

BORIS BECKER

The former Wimbledon, US Open and Australian Open champion loves the smell of babies.

Cherry Marmalade Haribo No. 5

LEWIS HAMILTON

Mercedes millionaire Hamilton has a weakness for a certain brand of sweets. He said, 'The smell of sweets. When you open a pack of cherry marmalade Haribo – this is the smell.'

SEBASTIAN COE

The former Olympic champion told the *Guardian* he loves the smell of 'a late jazz club'.

'a late jazz club'

'We're definitely going to get Brooklyn christened, but we don't know into which religion.'

David Beckham

'Hockey is a sport for white men. Basketball is a sport for black men. Golf is a sport for white men dressed like pimps.'

TIGER WOODS

COSMETIC TREATMENT

Sports stars are prone to keeping up appearances whatever the cost. Check out our selection of the best procedures:

WAYNE ROONEY

Wazza copped a great deal of hassle from fans and team-mates alike for hair transplant treatment that is rumoured to have cost £30,000. The Manchester United striker was pictured leaving a Harley Street clinic and he later revealed it was for a hair transplant where hairs are transplanted from donor areas, usually at the lower back of the head, and then replanted in affected areas. According to the clinic, the treatment is a 'major advance over older hair transplantation procedures that used larger grafts' and often produced an 'unnatural look'.

PETER CROUCH

Rooney's fellow England striker Crouch had cosmetic surgery on his nose in 2007 when he was playing for Liverpool. He was forced into the £4,000 procedure after he received a kick from Sheffield United's Rob Hulse in a Premier League game in 2007.

SHANE WARNE

Warnie has admitted to or is rumoured to have had several cosmetic procedures down the years to keep Mother Nature at bay. He spent £1,000 to have his teeth whitened. However, he attributes his new face post-retirement to moisturising and organic goji berry shakes.

BEST EVER

JOBS OUTSIDE OF SPORT

It's easy to forget that sports stars once trod in the same shoes as the rest of us. Some came to sport late after testing out the job market, while others went on to interesting careers in retirement. Here's a spread of our favourites:

JOSÉ MOURINHO

Before becoming 'The Special One' and managing the likes of Real Madrid and Chelsea to glory, José was a PE teacher in his native Portugal.

Old habits die hard for José, and if the Chelsea team forget their kit he makes them play in their vest and pants.

RORY & TONY UNDERWOOD

Brothers Rory and Tony both played on the wing for England at rugby and combined it with being RAF pilots.

Rory is the more fondly remembered of the two – partly because he's England's record try scorer and partly because he never had New Zealand's Jonah Lomu run over the top of him, like he was a welcome mat.

STEVE SAVIDAN

Former Monaco and France striker Steve Savidan spent a long time trying to make it to the top of the professional game – in fact, at one stage things were going so badly as a lower league player, he had to supplement his wages by working as a bin man.

His experience at getting rid of rubbish stood him in good stead, however, for the time he played against Titus Bramble.

ADAM HOLLIOAKE

Former England one-day captain Adam Hollioake took up mixed martial arts cage fighting in 2012 when he quit cricket.

After his first bout, he said, 'I had more adrenaline out there in one night than I did in 17 years of cricket.' In fairness, Adam, that's not hard. My nan's sudoku nights are more of a thrill ride than anything that's happened at Surrey in recent years.

STUART PEARCE

Stuart Pearce hasn't only been a tough tackler and a crappy manager during his career because in his early days at Coventry City he continued to do electrician work on the side.

He gave it up as his career took off, which is probably just as well. You don't really want someone nicknamed 'Psycho' to be prowling round the place armed with a screwdriver.

ALEX FERGUSON

Before signing for Rangers old red nose had an apprenticeship in the Glasgow dockyards.

He was a tool-maker – and no, that doesn't mean he created Anderson.

PETER SCHMEICHEL

Peter Schmeichel loved playing for Alex Ferguson so much he even adopted his trademark red nose. It wasn't all smooth sailing for him, though – before he made it in football he had a variety of jobs in his native Denmark, including working as a carpet fitter, selling advertising space and working in a charity shop.

Rumour has it that it was whilst at the charity shop that he met most of the Aston Villa team he played in – they were in rubbish bags and dumped outside the door overnight.

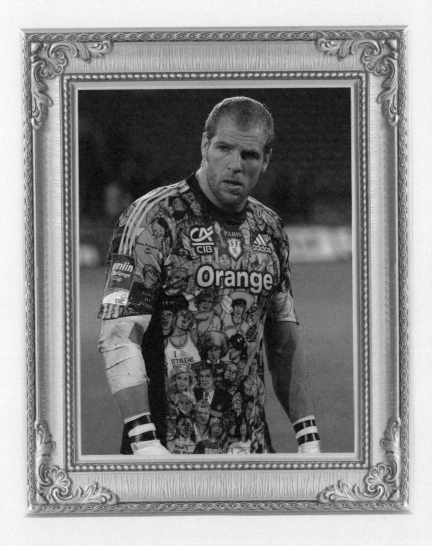

Here's James in his old Stade Français kit. We think we've found Wally just below his belly button

JAMES HASKELL

BORN: 2 April 1985, Windsor, England
PLAYER: Wasps, Stade Français, Ricoh Black Rams, Highlanders and England

1) Haskell was an early bloomer, becoming Wasps' youngest Premiership player in 2002 against Harlequins aged just 18. He advanced quickly in the England U21s too as the only player to have played every one of the 20 games for that age group two years running.

2) The Windsor native made his full England début against Wales in the 2007 Six Nations, part of an unprecedented Wasps back row. After a spell in the international wilderness during his three-year club spell overseas, Haskell was brought back in time for the 2015 World Cup.

3) On a visit to girlfriend Chloe Madeley's house, apparently her mum, Judy Finnegan, said if Chloe didn't marry him, then she would. And I bet he thought he'd seen some scary sights on the bottom of a ruck.

4) The Hask is a huge shooting fan and often retreats to the countryside. Not surprisingly for someone so staggeringly confident in himself, he claims he is really quite good at it. His top tip is to 'be relaxed'. That's easy for him to say – he's the one with the gun.

DID YOU KNOW: 'The King of Chatmandu', as he calls himself, has a few hidden talents, including being a juggler. Whether this had a hand in Stuart Lancaster bringing him back into the England fold we'll never know, but it beats Chris Ashton's dwarf tossing.

Feuds have kept the punters entertained for centuries now, and the combustible nature of the sporting arena is no different. Here's our pick of the best when the touchpaper was lit.

ROBERTO MANCINI AND MARIO BALOTELLI

The two Italians did not always see eye to eye when they were paired together as manager and striker at Manchester City. Balotelli lunged at Scott Sinclair in training once, leading to Mancini ordering him off the pitch. Naturally Balo refused and the two grappled before coaching staff separated them. Mancini said afterwards, 'For two seconds [I lost my temper], yes. During three, four seconds because he didn't want to leave the pitch, but for me he should because he can't do [this] against no one.' The former Sampdoria striker added, 'I don't speak with him every day, otherwise I would need a psychologist.'

Two-time world champion Hamilton got the wrong end of the stick when he thought fellow Briton Button had unfollowed him on Twitter. Hamilton tweeted to his 1 million plus followers: 'Just noticed @jensonbutton unfollowed, thats a shame. After 3 years as teammates, I thought we respected one another but clearly he doesn't.' He backtracked about an hour later saying, 'My bad, just found out Jenson never followed me. Don't blame him! Need to be on Twitter more!' The Mercedes driver later vowed to be more careful on social media in future.

DWAYNE JOHNSON AND JOHN CENA

Wrestlers John Cena and Dwayne 'The Rock' Johnson feuded with each other for around one year. 'The Rock' began the feud by calling Cena a 'big fat bowl of Fruity Pebbles', later adding that Cena's clothing made him look like a 'homeless Power Ranger' and 'Vanilla Ice'. Cena fuelled the fire by saying that he would never leave wrestling for such a long time to pursue an acting career like 'The Rock'. It all climaxed with 'The Rock' defeating Cena at Wrestlemania XXVIII.

Here's Ian showing that if you put any ex-footballer in
a wall they immediately protect their genitals

IAN HOLLOWAY

BORN: 12 March 1963, Kingswood, Bristol, England
PLAYER: Bristol Rovers, Wimbledon, Brentford, Torquay and QPR
MANAGER: Bristol Rovers, QPR, Plymouth Argyle, Leicester City, Blackpool, Crystal Palace and Millwall

1) Holloway started as an apprentice at his hometown club Bristol Rovers and enjoyed a productive four years patrolling the right flank before Wimbledon swooped for him in 1985. London wasn't for him, though, and he returned to Rovers for a second spell in 1987.
2) Under fledgling boss Gerry Francis, Holloway flourished, leading to an impressive spell at QPR and final return to Rovers in 1996 where he took on the player-manager role. He has since enjoyed a rather seesaw reputation as a boss, depending on which fans you talk to.
3) When he took the reins at Blackpool, the Holloway family brought their 33 chickens, three horses, two dogs and two ducks north with them. The club groundsman gifted them seven turkeys as well, one of whom later got a run-out in the first team under José Riga in 2014.
4) Holloway cheekily warned incoming Palace boss Tony Pulis about making a move on his wife after he replaced him. In his trademark style, he joked: 'Tony Pulis has moved into my house in London. He might have my old car as well, but he won't get my woman.'

DID YOU KNOW: Ian is so famed for his witty soundbites he's even released a book of quotes. Some fans claim that he only gets jobs because he has a wacky persona and says funny things – so in many ways he'd be better suited to being Mayor of London.

GIFTS TO SELF

Even though sporting gods are usually up to their tonsils with cash and free gifts, they occasionally like to treat themselves. Discover what fancy things these stars snapped up.

JENSON BUTTON

The former F1 world champion swooped for an antique samurai sword when he was in a Kuala Lumpur market during the Malaysian Grand Prix. The McLaren driver said: 'I don't know how old it is. I was looking around an antique shop in Malaysia and thought, "Ooh, that looks nice." It is an amazing bit of kit but I am maybe going to give it to Jessica to find out if it is real or not. I have wanted one since seeing Tom Cruise in *The Last Samurai*.'

MARIO BALOTELLI

The Italian has made a string of rash purchases in recent years, including treating himself to a Harley-Davidson motorcycle. Boss Roberto Mancini, though, banned the former Manchester City striker from driving it for insurance reasons so it picked up dust in the garage instead.

NANI

The former Manchester United winger clearly loves looking at himself as he has a life-size marble statue of himself in his living room. Not only that, the Portuguese international has topped it off with a jester-style hat given by a fan and football medals around his neck.

BEST EVER

CRY BABIES

Sport is all about drama and on the big occasions a mighty bottom lip tremble to put the enormity of what just happened into perspective. We've singled out a few moments when sports stars let their poker face slip and the floodgates opened in dramatic fashion:

JOHN TERRY – UEFA CHAMPIONS LEAGUE FINAL, MOSCOW, 2008

Chelsea captain John Terry slipped as he took a penalty in the shoot-out that would've won the Champions League for Chelsea against Manchester United.

And so another penalty shoot-out ended in tears for an England player. John's since made up for it, though, by putting on his kit and sneaking into every celebration from Chelsea's 2012 victory to the *Loose Women*'s *TV Quick* award.

ANDY MURRAY – VARIOUS

Win or lose, Andy Murray seems to end up in tears – including helping Britain through in the 2015 Davis Cup, winning Olympic gold and losing the US Open. In fact, sensitive Andy cries so often I can't think of the last time I saw him without red eyes and a snot bubble coming out of his nose.

The most memorable occasion, perhaps, was when he lost the 2012 Wimbledon final to Roger Federer and cried so hard the ground staff pulled the covers on.

MARION JONES – *THE OPRAH WINFREY SHOW*, 2008, ADMITTING TO STEROID ABUSE

US sprinter Marion Jones was stripped of the three Olympic gold medals she won in Sydney after admitting she took steroids.

Marion was eventually jailed for six months for lying about the drug abuse but melted hearts when she broke down in tears on *Oprah*. At least we think they were tears – it may've just been the steroids leaking out.

MIKA HÄKKINEN – ITALIAN GRAND PRIX, MONZA, 1999

Upon crashing in the 1999 Italian Grand Prix, Mika Häkkinen created an iconic moment as he hid behind a hedge to cry about it.

Mika thought the accident would not only end his hopes of winning the Drivers' Championship that year but also mean Sheilas' Wheels would take away his no claims bonus.

OLIVER MCCALL – WBC HEAVYWEIGHT BOUT V LENNOX LEWIS, 1997

Boxer Oliver McCall got himself so wound up ready for his title defence against Brit Lennox Lewis he entered the ring in tears.

In fairness, if I was about to receive several 1,600 PSI punches to the skull from Lennox I think I'd be soiling my shorts, let alone crying.

The referee stopped the fight in the fifth round with Lennox well on top and Oliver in tears. Oliver became the only boxer to lose a fight because he 'needed his mummy'.

HOW TO

BECOME A PREMIERSHIP RUGBY PLAYER

Rugby used to be an amateur sport, with players clocking in to bog-standard jobs like accountancy or insurance salesman before suiting up at weekends and grabbing testicles. Money has infiltrated the noble game now, with Premiership teams coughing up decent salaries. How could you join them?

If you've got a face like a well-chewed toffee and fancy getting the ears to match, rugby's the game for you.

Check if you're fat – if the answer's yes become a front row forward.

You need supreme courage, skill, tactical nous and the desire to hold another man without telling him you love him for 80 minutes.

Act like a homophobe but take part in an initiation so gay it would make most members of a gentlemen's sauna wince.

Punch each other repeatedly in the face until the final whistle goes, when you shake hands and agree to have a pint afterwards.

'I'm tired of hearing about money, money, money, money, money. I just want to play the game, drink Pepsi, wear Reebok.'

Shaquille O'Neal

JENNY JONES

BORN: 3 July 1980, Downend, Bristol, England
CAREER HIGHLIGHTS: Olympic bronze and three-time Winter X Games gold medallist

1) Having flown the winter sports flag for Britain almost single-handedly for several years as a three-time slopestyle Winter X Games champion, Jones pocket-rocketed her way into national treasure status after winning bronze medal at the 2014 Sochi Winter Olympic Games.

2) Sochi provided TV viewers back home in Blighty with a classic weepy moment when Jones spotted her mum and dad in the crowd moments after completing her medal-winning run. She had previously banned her parents from attending as it made her too nervous.

3) After winning bronze, she partied hard following four months sober. It only took two vodkas to make crowd surfing in the club seem a good idea. She revealed, 'The medal got pretty scratched from partying.' The mind boggles as to what the state she'd be in if she landed gold.

DID YOU KNOW: Having been a virtual unknown, after winning bronze Jenny appeared on seven national newspaper front pages. You could say she became an overnight celebrity. She then took a job on Channel 4's *The Jump*, so she quickly went back to not being one.

Jenny is the first Briton ever to win a medal on snow – although fans of successful Scottish football teams do query this.

Jenny originally learnt her snowboard skills as a chalet maid in France. She was talent spotted and entered global competitions with a group of young snowboarders dubbed the 'Fridge Kids'. The film *Chalet Girl* is rumoured to be based on her early exploits.

And here's Jenny auditioning for *E.T.*

INSPIRATIONS

A large part of success in sport is self-confidence: knowing it all, believing in yourself, maxing the envelope, etc. However, here are a few humbler ones who put their success down to outside forces:

RORY MCILROY

Sir Alex Ferguson proved to be an inspiration to Major winner McIlroy after he blew his first big chance with a final-round collapse at the 2011 Masters. Fergie sent him a text and the Northern Irishman revealed, 'It basically said I was in the same position as Rafael, who had been sent off against Bayern Munich in the match that saw United go out of the Champions League. I was amazed and honoured. He said there were a lot of similarities between me and Rafael because we are both promising young players who had made mistakes. We just needed to soak up the lessons that had taught us and come back stronger than ever. To get a text like that from Sir Alex just a couple of days after he and the club had suffered such a big disappointment was right out of the blue. It stopped me feeling sorry for myself and I knew I had to get back out on the course quickly and show what I'm really capable of.'

ENGLAND RUGBY UNION

Sky football pundit Gary Neville was brought in by England rugby union coach Stuart Lancaster to try and lift the team after the poor 2011 World Cup performance and 'unsavoury' off-pitch PR disasters. Neville drew on the spirit of Euro 1996 and England's famous run at home in a bid to turn the players' mindsets around. Lancaster said: 'I am trying to remind the players about the pride and honour and standing of being an international rugby player in this country; it is massive. When Gary Neville says it is an honour, it is an honour. And if the players understand that, then you get more responsible behaviour as well.'

ARSÈNE WENGER

Arsenal's studious manager used the inspiration of Barack Obama's US presidential win to rouse his own players during the 2011/12 season as they fought to shake off a trophy drought. He claimed that the election proved that there is no obstacle to success for the genuinely talented when he said: 'I've always fought for the idea in sport that, if you have the necessary quality, then you play. Right now we have the example of Barack Obama in the United States, where everybody is really happy because he has made it to the very top.'

BEST EVER

It might come as a surprise to many, but the more successful you are as a sports star, the more likely it seems you fall prey to bizarre superstitions. So what routines do the great and good trot out?

BJÖRN BORG

Five-time Wimbledon champion Björn Borg had a superstition of always wearing the same shirt and never shaving during a tournament.

When he won a final, he'd pull off his shirt and throw it into the crowd to celebrate.

Given his later career, the biggest surprise is that Björn didn't have lucky pants.

TURK WENDELL

Former New York Mets relief pitcher Turk Wendell had a huge list of superstitions he felt he had to adhere to. These included not treading on the baselines, chewing black liquorice and even brushing his teeth between innings.

He also wore a necklace made out of teeth from animals he'd hunted and killed – but they never brought the animals much luck! Because Turk's lucky number is 99 he asked for his salary to be $9,999,999.99 – similarly I told the publisher of this book that my lucky number was 1M. So they told me to sod off that many times.

GARY LINEKER

Mexico '86 Golden Boot winner Gary Lineker admitted to several superstitions – including never shooting during the warm-up for fear he'd use up his goals before the game started.

He might be right as I've often seen Andy Carroll cracking them in during the warm-up.

NASCAR

There's a superstition right across Nascar that no one can have peanut shells on the track. But who's throwing peanut shells out of a car? Donkey Kong?

MOISÉS ALOU

Former San Francisco Giants outfielder Moisés Alou never wore gloves when batting and admitted that he brought himself luck and hardened his hands by urinating on them.

It also made him the least 'high-fived' man in the history of American sport.

NEIL MCKENZIE

South African opening batsman Neil McKenzie was once pranked by his team-mates, who taped his bat to the ceiling. After he got it down and scored a century he continued to tape it to the roof before every game.

Because being the victim of a prank brought him success Neil also asked his team-mates to wedgie him, put dog muck in his hood and hide rotting fish in his car.

TIGER WOODS

During his golfing career Tiger Woods has won 14 Major titles – which he puts down in part to his superstition of wearing a red shirt on the final day.

It may sound daft but in fairness it's hard to think of anyone who's spent more time 'getting lucky' than Tiger.

Here's Zlatan the day he found out that if you forget your kit
Sweden make you play in your bra and pants

ZLATAN IBRAHIMOVIĆ

BORN: 3 October 1981, Malmö, Sweden
PLAYER: Malmö, Ajax, Juventus, Inter Milan, Barcelona, AC Milan, Paris Saint-Germain and Sweden

1) The most expensive footballer in history through combined transfers was very nearly lost to the football world when he considered quitting in his teens to work in the Malmö docks. His manager convinced him to carry on and he did well enough to earn a transfer to Ajax.
2) After impressing in Holland, Zlatan moved to Italy and started with a mixed spell at Juventus before truly becoming a global star in Inter's Serie A winning side. Further stints at Barcelona, Milan and PSG all ended in domestic league titles for the talismanic Swede.
3) A search engine has been created in the vein of Google called http://zlaaatan.com/ that helps bolster the charismatic striker's online domination, while the verb 'to Zlatan', which refers to an outlandishly talented action, has been added to the Swedish dictionary to boot.
4) Zlatan claimed a dressing-room speech from a half-naked Fabio Capello turned him into the superstar striker he is now during their prolific time together at Juventus. Sadly for England fans, the Golden Generation didn't take too kindly to Fabio flashing his moobs in their own quest.

DID YOU KNOW: Ibracadabra's dream dinner party involves him, his girlfriend, Hollywood legend Al Pacino and football maverick Diego Maradona. I'd love to see what scores they'd give him in the taxis on the way home.

SPORTING ASTEROIDS

Now, of course, one of the greatest honours in life is having an asteroid named after you. So, which famous sporting asteroids take the longest to orbit the sun, then?

RAFAEL NADAL
128036 Rafaelnadal is a main belt asteroid discovered in 2003 at the Observatorio Astronómico de Mallorca and named after Majorca-born Nadal. It takes 3.77 years to orbit.

LANCE ARMSTRONG
12373 Lancearmstrong is a main belt asteroid discovered by Charles de Saint-Aignan at Lowell Observatory examining films taken at Palomar when he was in California. It was named after disgraced Texan cyclist Armstrong during the 'peak' of his career and takes 3.84 years to orbit the sun.

ARSÈNE WENGER
33179 Arsènewenger is a main belt asteroid with an orbital period of 4.23 years. The asteroid was discovered on 29 March 1998 by Ian P. Griffin, who is naturally a fan of Arsenal.

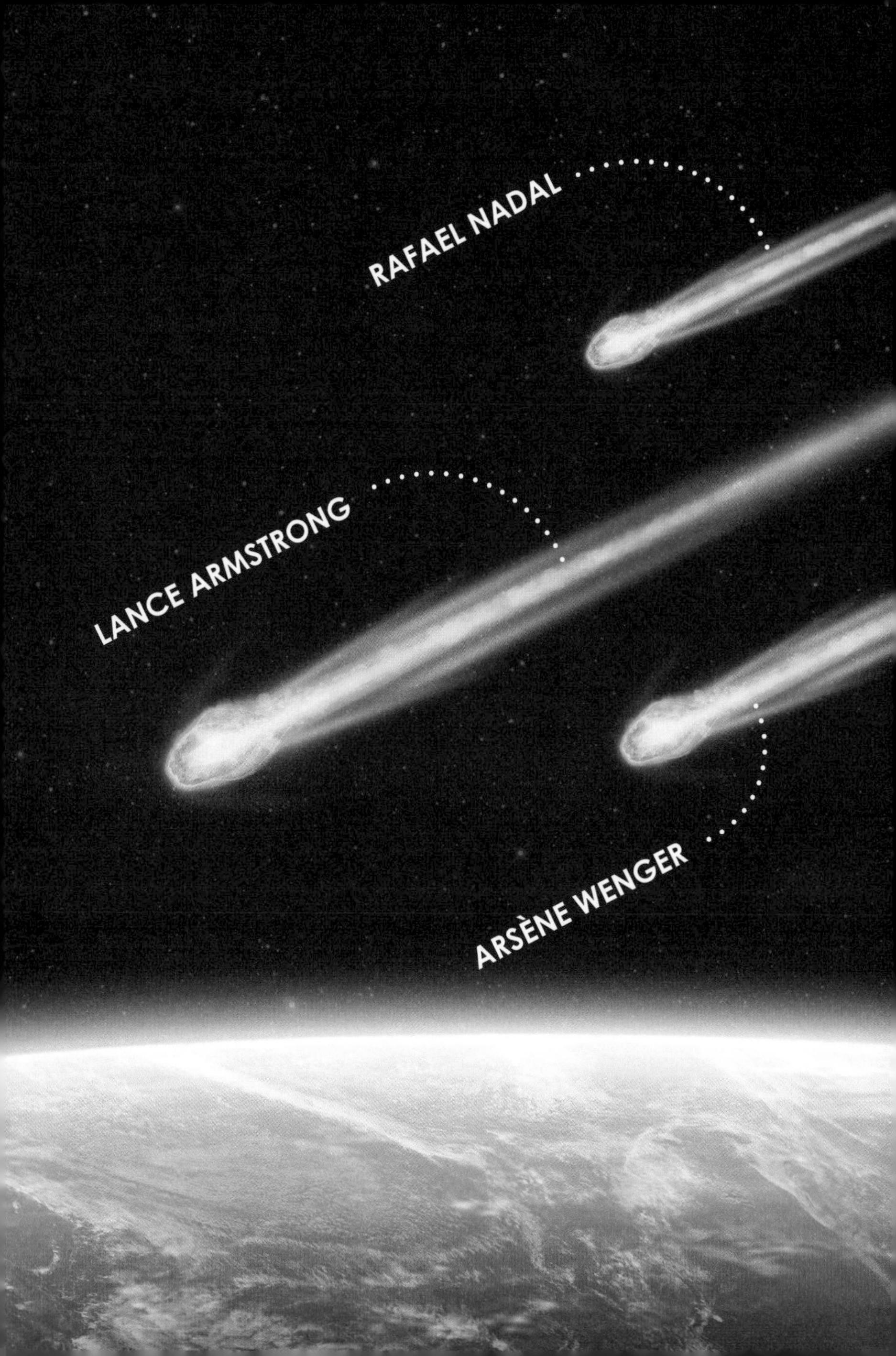
RAFAEL NADAL
LANCE ARMSTRONG
ARSÈNE WENGER

CHRIS KAMARA

BORN: 25 December 1957, Middlesbrough, England
PLAYER: Portsmouth, Swindon Town, Brentford, Stoke City, Leeds United, Luton Town, Sheffield United and Bradford
MANAGER: Bradford and Stoke City

1) Kamara's eclectic journey around the leagues as a player saw two stints at Portsmouth and Swindon, with the tough-tackling midfielder enjoying his best spell when helping the Robins to two successive promotions before he wound down his career as player-coach at Bradford.

2) The former Royal Navy stoker took over at Bradford as manager in 1995 and managed to carve out a decent few years on the back of a canny eye in the transfer market. One season as Stoke boss followed before it became apparent he was more suited to TV punditry at Sky.

3) Kammy's reputation for on-air gaffes has seen him become a cult figure on *Gillette Soccer Saturday* with his catchphrase 'Unbelievable, Jeff' a particular fan favourite. His capacity for buffoonery has even extended to comedy skits in recent Ladbrokes betting adverts.

4) He caught a street robber in Brazil during some World Cup downtime and posted images of it all unfolding on Twitter. After successfully giving chase, the former midfield maestro tweeted, 'Not lost me pace!!! I just caught this street robber. Done in now though.'

DID YOU KNOW: Before the 2010 World Cup a Facebook campaign got Kamara to change his name by deed poll to Chris Cabanga – 'cabanga' means 'imagine' in Zulu – as in 'Imagine what's just happened on the pitch whilst you've been looking in the wrong direction'.

Unbelievably in the bottomless pit that is the Premier League, clubs have resorted to pinching the pennies to cut costs instead of capping player wages. Check out these humdingers.

FULHAM

There's nothing like a good chicken and egg story to tickle us, with the Cottagers providing a humdinger to keep everyone amused. The club bought eight chickens in 2012 to keep at their Motspur Park training ground in the hope they would save on catering costs. The club used it as a fun way to engage their fans on social media via the #fulhamchickens hashtag, with 3,000 tweets suggesting names for the chickens. The names eventually picked were Martin Jolk, Mark Squawkzer, George CoHen, Brede Hengelend, Chickson Etuhu, Rooster Dembele, Cock-a-Doodle Deuce (Clint Dempsey's nickname is Deuce) and Pavel Peckgrobnyak.

CHELSEA

Nearby neighbours Chelsea were looking to trim costs of their own in 2012, with the club eventually deciding that slashing free club haircuts could do the job. Then manager André Villas-Boas discovered the players, wives and families were all getting the expensive haircuts for free at the training ground and promptly stopped it in its tracks. Apparently, a specialist Afro hairdresser was even brought in from Brixton to style the black players before the axe.

ARSENAL

Arsène Wenger and his stingy backroom team put an end to shirt swapping at the end of Premier League games in 2007 due to the huge losses they were incurring when the likes of Thierry Henry and Robin van Persie kept swapping with rivals after the games. They were still allowed, though, to swap shirts after Champions League and FA Cup matches.

BEST EVER

EXCUSES

One of the many pleasures sports fans have following their teams or athletes comes when a manager or athlete finds wonderful excuses for tough losses or moments of madness. It makes news editors ecstatic and makes us howl with laughter, so check out these corking excuses:

GREY DAY

When Manchester United were trailing 3–0 to an average Southampton side at half-time in 1996, Alex Ferguson made the decision to change the side's new grey strip because he felt the players couldn't see each other properly. Jamie Redknapp knows how Fergie feels. He's been having trouble with grey for decades now.

TIGHT-FITTING CLOTHES

Whilst we're on fashion: Sri Lanka lost the ICC Champions Trophy final to Pakistan and did not blame their performance for the loss … they blamed tight clothes.

LUIS SUÁREZ BITING

Yes, after the third time of being caught out biting an opponent, Luis Suárez decided to go for an excuse doctors have heard many times before … the old 'slipped and fell onto it' excuse.

After he plunged his teeth into Giorgio Chiellini's shoulder during the 2014 World Cup, Suárez said: 'I lost my balance, making my body unstable and falling on top of my opponent. At that moment I hit my face against the player, leaving a small bruise on my cheek and a strong pain in my teeth.' He was banned from football for four months.

I GOT DISTRACTED BY A STREAKER

At the best-of-19 Masters snooker final at Wembley in 1997, Ronnie O'Sullivan was leading 8–3 when a streaker came into the arena. He would then go on to lose seven straight games and the match.

Sounds like something that would affect a 15-year-old.

LASAGNE-GATE

Spurs blamed a dodgy lasagne for defeat to West Ham on the final day of the 2005/06 Premier League season which denied them a Champions League spot. Ten players went down with a stomach bug that destroyed their top four hopes. We're not sure why Spurs keep missing out on the top four, but maybe they had a bad bolognese in 2013, some rotten ravioli in 2014 and an off quattro formaggi in 2015.

NOT ENOUGH BALL BOYS

During his days at Real Madrid José Mourinho blamed a Supercopa loss against Barcelona on a lack of ball boys. 'There were no ball boys in the second half,' he said before adding that it's 'something typical of small teams' like Barcelona. Ouch.

BOUNCY BALLS

As we're on the subject of balls, after Newcastle United suffered a humiliating 3–1 loss to Stevenage in the 1998 FA Cup, manager Kenny Dalglish knew what was at fault: 'The balls were too bouncy,' he said. He went on to say the crowd were too noisy, the grass was too green and the referee was too blind!

MISSING MICHAEL

Arsenal have Henry, United have Fergie … Fulham had Michael Jackson.

We were all surprised when Fulham's former owner Mohamed Al-Fayed decided to put up a statue of Michael Jackson outside the ground, but after they were relegated he blamed it on the new owner's decision to remove the 'lucky' statue. 'This statue was a charm and we removed the luck from the club and now we have to pay the price,' he said.

I think we are all paying the price in not being able to see that amazing statue outside Craven Cottage any more.

SLIM TONIC MISTAKE

Kolo Touré was slapped with a six-month ban for failing a drug test for which he blamed his wife's diet pills. Although he's stopped taking the pills he can still wear his wife's dresses on Sundays.

AND FINALLY … MOST USED EXCUSE OF ALL TIME

Arsène Wenger's 'I didn't see it.'

HOW TO

BECOME A PROFESSIONAL WRESTLER

Wrestling has enjoyed two golden eras on either side of the pond; Big Daddy and Giant Haystacks keeping British audiences glued to the TV while gym rat behemoths battle it out in front of thousands Stateside. Here's how you can jump off corner posts with the best wherever you ply your trade:

If you're not into boxing but fancy a fight you've got three choices – join the police, if you like knees to the skull then take up cage fighting, or you can go into professional wrestling.

Wrestling gets criticised but don't forget it's a great excuse to shout all the time and entertain young children in your pants.

The first thing to do is to turn your body into something so muscular it looks like a carrier bag full of salami.

Choose yourself an original identity – here's a few that are up for grabs. 'The Sideboard', 'Trolley Collector' and 'Loneliest Loss Adjustor'.

Get told that what you do is fake – just after you've been thrown onto your head by an 8ft man dressed as a voodoo conjurer, then hit with a chair.

Enjoy a career at the very top – for about six years until the steroids make your heart explode.

Roy once tried to soften his image with a cheap PR stunt ...

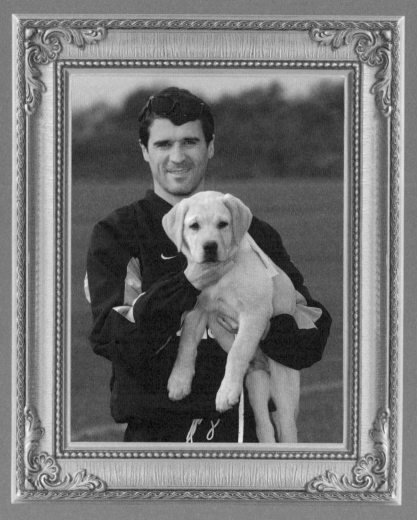

... sadly, that's the last known photograph of that dog alive

ROY KEANE

BORN: 10 August 1971, Cork, Ireland
PLAYER: Nottingham Forest, Manchester United, Celtic and
Republic of Ireland
MANAGER: Sunderland, Ipswich Town, Republic of Ireland
(assistant) and Aston Villa (assistant)

1) Keane grew up supporting Celtic and Tottenham and was spotted
playing for Cobh Ramblers in a youth match by a Forest scout. Dugout
king Brian Clough liked what he saw of the combative midfielder on
trial and brought him over for the princely sum of £47,000.
2) After helping Forest to the FA Cup final in 1991 where they lost to
boyhood club Spurs, Alex Ferguson cunningly beat Blackburn to his
signature for a then British transfer record fee of £3.75 million. Keane
soon became the focal point of incredible success at Old Trafford.
3) The Irishman revealed he turned down the chance to appear in *Big
Brother* and the jungle on *I'm a Celebrity … Get Me Out of Here*. The latter
is a big ask for anyone, but it would have been amusing watching him
pick a fight with himself in an empty room during the former.
4) Keane admitted that when United played Sporting Lisbon in a
friendly, John O'Shea was made dizzy by Cristiano Ronaldo, which
was when Keane realised how good Ronaldo was. Not the greatest test,
though, to be fair. O'Shea makes Andros Townsend look like Messi.

DID YOU KNOW: FIFA Vice President Jack Warner once claimed
Keane was disrespectful towards small countries, to which Keano
responded by calling the now disgraced official 'a clown'. Warner is
now available for children's birthday parties after leaving his FIFA post.

MOST CONDOMS

The Olympics are well known for serving up golds, silvers, bronzes and heartbreak, but also two weeks where fit athletes get jiggy en masse. Which Games then produced the most rubbers?

SYDNEY 2000 OLYMPICS

After the original 50,000 condoms provided for the Sydney competitors were quickly used up in the Olympic village, the organisers rushed in another 20,000 for the horny athletes. That measures up at a staggering 51 condoms per athlete, with javelin exponent Breaux Greer revealing to *Men's Journal*, 'There's a lot of sex going on. You get a lot of people who are in shape and, you know, testosterone's up and everybody's attracted to everybody.'

ATHENS 2004 OLYMPICS

The Greek organisers handed out 130,000 free condoms thanks to suppliers Durex, with 30,000 sachets of lubricant for good measure; that's 12 condoms and three sachets per athlete overall.

BEIJING 2008 OLYMPICS

Chinese organisers supplied 100,000 free condoms to the Olympic competitors, leaving the figure at a disappointing nine each as 5,000 condoms were left over at the end of the Games.

Just because Floyd's the best boxer in the world doesn't
mean he doesn't get scared of being Home Alone

FLOYD MAYWEATHER, JR

BORN: 24 February 1977, Grand Rapids, Michigan, USA
CAREER HIGHLIGHTS: Olympic bronze + WBA, WBC, IBF and WBO champion

1) Young Floyd followed his boxer father Floyd Sr into the sweet science and he's claimed that his grandmother saw his potential first. After a troubled childhood, he found solace in the gym and went on to represent the USA at the 1996 Olympics, where he won feather bronze.
2) 'Pretty Boy' won his first world title at super featherweight against Genaro Hernandez two years into his pro career. The next 17 years saw Floyd sweep up several more at five weights including famous wins over Oscar De La Hoya, Ricky Hatton and Manny Pacquiao.
3) Victor Ortiz headbutted Mayweather in their WBC welter clash, with the ref docking Ortiz a point. Ortiz hugged Floyd to apologise, only for Mayweather to hammer his opponent with a vicious two-punch combination that knocked his compatriot down for the win. Classy.
4) Mayweather is notorious for splashing the cash. He won $827,273 by placing a $350,000 bet on boxers Gennady Golovkin and Willy Monroe plus a basketball game. Mayweather posted on Instagram, 'I'm getting paid while watching others entertain and perform.'

DID YOU KNOW: 'Money' Mayweather celebrated his birthday by signing a new $200 million TV contract – he should've checked the small print, though, because it meant he'd agreed to appear on the next series of *Celebrity Coach Trip*.

PERFORMANCE ENHANCER

Most of us need a pick-me-up every now and then to maintain our form at work, play or in the bedroom – sports stars are no different. Explore our bizarre selection of remedies:

PHIL TAYLOR

'The Power' was looking for ways to stay lighter on his feet in a bid to keep his incredible run at major tournaments going on the darts circuit. The 16-time world champion revealed: 'When we were in Bournemouth, I was tempted to take my shoes and socks off and go for a paddle – but then a friend suggested trying a fish pedicure. So I've had my feet in a fish tank, and all these little piranhas made a meal of them. Afterwards you feel like your feet can dance like Fred Astaire. Admittedly the fish can't manage a nine-dart finish, but if it helps me to feel relaxed on stage, all that tickling will have been worthwhile.'

DAVID HAYE

The British boxer wedged out an incredible £1,500 a week in the run-up to his domestic heavyweight clash with Audley Harrison, with kangaroo meat top of the menu. His diet, which was devised by top nutritionist Ruben Tavares, also included flying fish, blue cabbage and yellow beetroot, while Haye claimed that the kangaroo put an extra spring in his step.

PARK JI SUNG

The South Korean's prodigious engine could partly be attributed to drinking frog juice in his childhood. He did not realise what it was at the time and revealed: 'It smelled like intestines, as if deadly and undrinkable. I know now that I ate frogs. If it was good for my body, I ate a lot. I'd sometimes throw up after eating but still I ate what I was given. I wanted to be good at football and my desire was greater than my distaste at eating these foods.'

Here's Rory getting some bad news from the Invisible Man

RORY MCILROY

BORN: 4 May 1989, Holywood, Northern Ireland
CAREER HIGHLIGHTS: Two-time PGA champion, Open champion
+ US Open champion

1) McIlroy got the golf fever from his father Gerry and became the youngest club member at their local Holywood course aged just seven. He helped Europe win the Junior Ryder Cup at 15, made his European Tour début at 16 and won the amateur Silver Medal at the 2007 Open.

2) Rors turned professional in September 2007, but it took him four years until he got into proper Major contention. His final-round collapse at the 2011 Masters was followed by a huge US Open victory two months later and further Majors at the US PGA and Open.

3) Graeme McDowell gave him the nickname BMW. McIlroy's fellow US Open winner explained, 'We nicknamed him BMW because he is the ultimate driving machine. He's probably the best driver of the ball I've ever seen.' Shame, as Skoda has a better ring to it.

4) McIlroy was surprised by pop stars JLS at his US Open celebration party in Holywood. He said, 'I didn't know anything about it. I just saw this car coming down the driveway and I thought "Who are these guys?"' You often see JLS at parties – mostly waitering nowadays.

DID YOU KNOW: Wee Mac's main mentor is Jack Nicklaus. Rory was told by 'The Golden Bear' that 'I needed to be a little more arrogant on the golf course and think a little bit more about myself.' McIlroy duly ended his engagement to Caroline Wozniacki by phone. Nice.

PET HATES

Some sport stars are known for splitting hairs due to their single-minded desire to be the best. What really gets under their skin, then, when push comes to shove?

PHIL TAYLOR

'The Power' has a couple of things that get on his wick. Asked what he would put in Room 101, the 16-time world darts champion revealed: 'Rucksacks! I hate 'em. I hate 'em with a passion. On aeroplanes, people walking past with rucksacks knocking me on the back of the head.' As for arrows in general, he also added that he dislikes whistlers in the crowd.

JONNY WILKINSON

The rugby World Cup winner has stage fright, believe it or not. Asked what he would put in Room 101, the former England fly-half replied: 'I tell you what I'd put in: audience participation in things like stage shows or pantos. It scares the life out of me. I literally do not go to theatres and that type of thing because I'm convinced … well, in my history whenever anyone's been asked to do anything it's always been me.' He also can't stand people with bad attitudes, for good measure. He said, 'Never liked the "That's life", "You win some you lose some" outlook.'

JACK WILSHERE

Arsenal's mercurial midfielder has not exactly led a clean-cut life in the celebrity eye, so it will come as a surprise to learn that his pet hate is people not taking their shoes off indoors. He told *Match of the Day* magazine: 'When somebody comes into my house and doesn't take their shoes off! I had builders round recently and they were all walking around with shoes on – I had to put a sign up to tell them to get them off. In my house, it's shoes off!'

'Don't say I don't get along with my team-mates. I just don't get along with some of the guys on the team.'

Terrell Owens,
former NFL player

Here's José before he was a manager …

… coming third in a Lionel Ritchie look-a-like competition

JOSÉ MOURINHO

BORN: 26 January 1963, Setubal, Lisbon, Portugal
MANAGER: Benfica, Uniao de Leiria, Porto, Chelsea, Inter Milan and Real Madrid

1) Unless you've been living in a cave without wifi for the last decade or so, you will have heard of 'The Special One'. After a far from spectacular career as an eighties midfielder in Portugal, Mourinho got his big break as an interpreter to Bobby Robson at Sporting Lisbon.

2) Robson then took him to Porto and Barcelona, his chance to manage coming at Benfica in 2000. He eventually took over at rivals Porto, where he made his name with domestic trophies and a wild celebration in front of Fergie at Old Trafford en route to 2004 Champions League success.

3) When touring around Chelsea at one particular open-top bus parade, Mourinho attempted to serenade the crowd with a rendition of The Pensioners' 'Blue is the Colour'. His mangled attempt on the mike made Vic Reeves's club singer on *Shooting Stars* sound like Sinatra.

4) One of José's big favourites, Didier Drogba, revealed that the Portuguese charmer texts him at night whilst he sleeps. So long as it doesn't start with 'Bae, I'm all alone' we can't see the problem.

DID YOU KNOW: Actor Viggo Mortensen has disclosed his dislike for 'The Special One'. He revealed, 'There's a real character whom I loathe but find entertaining – José Mourinho.' Arsène Wenger agrees – apart from the 'but find entertaining' bit.

HOW TO

BECOME A CHAMPION JOCKEY

Horse racing still pulls in the loyal punters every day in the UK, with millions anxious to piss away or launder their hard-earned money. For jockeys, the years of eating air and sweating buckets result in a decent pay day, so check out you can boss the paddock banter:

If you're into sport and handy with a whip then your only choices are to become Formula 1 guru, Max Moseley's PA or a jockey.

However, you need to make sure you stop growing aged five and consider supermodels 'chubby'.

Remember, horse racing is dangerous – be prepared to spend nearly as much time in ambulances as Abou Diaby.

Choose your horse carefully – if it doesn't win then you want to ensure it'll be tasty for the post-race barbecue.

Beware that horses are often quite bitter. Even the ones that win the Grand National appear on the chat-show circuit almost as rarely as winners of *The Voice*.

Practise your flying dismount whenever you can – although remember to ask permission from whoever you're having sex with.

PRE-MATCH PREPARATION

Whether you're getting ready for a job interview or a big night out on the town, you have your habits to prepare for them. Are these lessons to be learned from sport's glitterati?

CRISTIANO RONALDO
CR7 had his hair and make-up touched up before Portugal's Euro 2012 clash against Holland.

ANDY MURRAY
The Scot prepared for his 2012 Wimbledon matches by playing *Goldeneye* on his N64.

ARSÈNE WENGER
Arsenal's boss once maintained six minutes of unbroken silence as a pre-match 'pep talk'.

'I would not be bothered if we lost every game as long as we won the league.'

MARK VIDUKA

Here's Ronnie with the world's most unsubtle snooker fan

RONNIE O'SULLIVAN

BORN: 5 December 1975, Wordsley, England
CAREER HIGHLIGHTS: Five World titles, five Masters titles and five UK Championships

1) O'Sullivan was destined for baize greatness from the age of ten when he made his first century break. 'The Rocket' backed this up with a maximum break in the final of the 1991 British Amateur Championship and duly turned professional the following year aged 16.

2) The Essex Exocet started out by winning 74 of his first 76 professional matches, but lost out in the first round of the 1993 World Championship. He did defeat Stephen Hendry, though, at the UK Championship to become the youngest winner of a ranking tournament.

3) Ronnie once revealed that after watching *Black Swan* he had considered getting his leg amputated and replacing it with a wooden leg. It's unconfirmed whether it would have a thin end that he could chalk.

4) Rocket was a vociferous supporter of the Labour Party during the 2015 general election. O'Sullivan was a regular at rallies and also posted selfies of himself with Ed Miliband on Twitter. Miliband probably should have focused on actual policies rather than Ronnie RTs.

DID YOU KNOW: O'Sullivan is pals with Rolling Stones guitarist Ronnie Wood and art's *enfant terrible* Damien Hirst. They were all spotted on a night out in 2008 that finished with snooker and a 145 O'Sullivan break. Well, that's what Ronnie remembers anyway.

BEST EVER

INJURIES

Sometimes we forget that sports stars are mere mortals like the rest of us, such is their magnificence in their chosen sphere. Thankfully, there is the odd moment when we get to revel in the type of everyday calamity that regularly befalls us. Here's a cracking selection:

ALEX STEPNEY

Alex Stepney famously shouted so violently at his Manchester United defence that he broke his own jaw. The most surprising thing about this was that Fábio da Silva wasn't playing in that team.

LEROY LITA

No place is safe for a sports star – not even tucked up under a duvet. Former Reading striker Leroy Lita was sidelined after a stretch went wrong in his bed and he pulled a muscle in his leg.

If you're looking for some more footballers with bed-related injuries, please purchase the X-rated version of this book.

ADAM EATON

The luckless baseball player Adam Eaton managed to do himself some serious damage opening a DVD with a knife in 2001. In trying to prise open the case, the San Diego Padres pitcher stabbed himself in the stomach. He made a full recovery, in case you're worried.

MARIO BALOTELLI

Madcap Mario suffered swelling to his face during a UEFA Cup match after he had an allergic reaction to the grass. Since moving to Liverpool he has also become allergic to scoring goals.

DIEGO MARADONA

Diego Maradona required ten stitches in his lip after he was bitten in the face by one of his dogs. We've looked into this and believe that he bought the hound from the Argentinian sniffer dog department.

DEREK PRINGLE

Former Essex and England cricketer Derek Pringle had to pull out of a 1980s Test match when he put his back out typing a letter. To any of our younger readers, a letter is a hard copy of a tweet.

PATRICE EVRA

During a Champions League semi-final Manchester United defender Patrice Evra injured his foot and needed nine stitches. The best thing about this, though, was that he put a chicken breast in his boot to help heal the injury, and after the match the chicken would be cooked … That's actually the Colonel's secret recipe.

PRE-SEASON TRAINING

The football season never seems to end these days thanks to the endless summer tours, so it's amazing teams have time for pre-season training. Here's our pick of the more unusual trips:

SOUTHAMPTON

Mauricio Pochettino has been a breath of fresh air since he brought his style of management to the Premier League with Southampton and Spurs. During the Saints' pre-season tour of Spain in 2013, the Argentian strolled across hot coals, with the players a touch more apprehensive. They were also shown how to break arrows with their collarbones.

ARSENAL

No hot rocks or peculiar racing tests for Arsenal head honcho Arsène Wenger and his troops on their more conventional pre-season tour. The former Nagoya Grampus Eight manager got a local chef to demonstrate to Mikel Arteta and Bacary Sagna instead how to slice up a huge tuna fish and teach the players the secret of the special rice used to make sushi.

LIVERPOOL

Brendan Rodgers put a novel spin on pre-season training in 2013 when his Liverpool players raced tuk-tuks in Thailand to try and get up to speed for the new season. Raheem Sterling and Jordan Henderson weaved around a car park to try and test their skill and agility, while a Bangkok restaurant made a kit out of coloured condoms in homage to their favourite team.

Here is Alan during a summer training camp at Newcastle

ALAN PARDEW

BORN: 18 July 1961, Wimbledon, London, England
PLAYER: Crystal Palace, Charlton Athletic and Barnet
MANAGER: Reading, West Ham, Charlton Athletic, Southampton, Newcastle United and Crystal Palace

1) Pards has the distinction of reaching the FA Cup final as a player and a manager, only to lose both. First, with Crystal Palace in 1990's Manchester United replay win that launched Fergie's Old Trafford career, then with the Hammers in 2006 when Stevie G's rocket propelled Liverpool to victory.
2) Alan was rewarded for a successful 2011–12 campaign that saw the Magpies just miss out on a Champions League place in fifth with a new eight-year contract. Owner Mike Ashley might as well have placed a voodoo curse on him as they plummeted to 16th next time out.
3) He once held an Australia-themed lunch as a tribute to Geordie legends Ant and Dec. Australian creatures were handled and everyone underwent bushtucker trials, although reports Ashley preferred eating bollocks rather than talking it are yet to be confirmed.
4) Pardew has a longstanding feud with Arsène Wenger that included a 2006 touchline fight – and to think people thought Pards wouldn't fit in at Newcastle.

DID YOU KNOW: Alan backed striker Shola Ameobi to become prime minster of his native Nigeria. After both left Tyneside, Pardew signed him for Palace but released him in June 2015. Ameobi was rumoured to be on his way to Hull next rather than high political office.

PRE-TOURNAMENT RELAXATION

With high stakes, high wages and high-pitched abuse, it's important to be at your best for the biggest games. Here's how the cream of the sporting world get themselves centred for the grand occasion:

MIKE TINDALL

The 2003 rugby World Cup winner did not have as much to prove on the international stage as his younger team-mates during the 2011 World Cup. Consequently, he warmed up for the tournament with a bungee jump and the now infamous 'Mad Midget Weekender' down in New Zealand. The *Sun* newspaper reported that the group were 'watching a light-hearted dwarf-throwing contest when scores of women made a beeline for the strapping lads'.

SIR ALEX FERGUSON

Ahead of the 2011 Champions League final clash with Barcelona at Wembley, Fergie took some of his Manchester United squad to watch the musical *Jersey Boys* in London 48 hours before the game. Sadly for them, it did not sprinkle any magic on them as they slumped to a 3–1 defeat.

NOVAK DJOKOVIC

The smooth Serb got ready for the 2011 Wimbledon at the All
England Club by befriending a squirrel in the garden of his rented
house as his pet poodle Pierre was not allowed to travel with him.
He tweeted, 'It's my best friend now in London, the little squirrel.'

Victoria hasn't really retired, she's just quit Team GB,
and signed for T'Yorkshire Cycling Team

VICTORIA PENDLETON

BORN: 24 September 1980, Stotfold, England
CAREER HIGHLIGHTS: Olympic, World, European and
Commonwealth gold medallist

1) Pendleton was spotted at 16 by an assistant national track coach
and combined a promising track career with her studies. She
made a name for herself on graduation with fourth at the 2002
Commonwealth Games, 2003 Worlds and 2004 Worlds in her
speciality sprint.

2) She broke her gold medal duck at the 2005 Worlds, which ushered
in a phenomenal spell that included two Olympic golds and a silver
medal across Beijing and London. It was her sprint domination at six
different World Championships that truly marked her out, though.

3) Victoria regularly has 'easy chicken night' with husband Scott
Gardner where they cook chicken breast on a George Foreman
grill. She said, 'It takes five minutes to cook and two minutes to
eat.' Pendleton's odds of winning *Celebrity Masterchef* were slashed in
seconds.

4) Pendleton attended sponsor parties after she retired at London 2012.
One such occasion was partying in Mahiki nightclub and she revealed
'this sweaty guy planted a big kiss on me in front of Scott'. Sven-Göran
Eriksson denies all knowledge he was in Mayfair that night.

DID YOU KNOW: Queen Victoria took on rugby team Sale Sharks in
a series of fitness tests including speed, endurance and weight-training
sessions. The Sharks players declared she was 'massively impressive'
then answered questions about her performance in the tests.

BEST EVER

INSULTS

Some sports stars try to gain a psychological edge with a cutting insult. Here are a few belters that have kept us entertained down the years:

MARCO MATERAZZI TO ZIDANE

We should probably begin with one of the most famous insults in sporting history. Italian footballer Marco Materazzi has finally revealed what he said to Zinedine Zidane to make the Frenchman headbutt him during the World Cup final. Marco claims: 'I was tugging his shirt, he said to me, "If you want my shirt so much I'll give it to you afterwards," I answered that I'd prefer his sister.'

TERRY NEILL TO OWN PLAYER

One morning during his time as manager of Arsenal, Terry Neill called across the pitch to one of his charges: 'You – every day in training you play worse than the day before. Today, you played like tomorrow.'

ROD MARSH AND IAN BOTHAM

In an Ashes match Ian Botham arrived at the wicket to a bit of cheek from the Aussie keeper Rod Marsh. Marsh went on to say: 'So how's your wife and my kids?' To which Botham quickly replied: 'Wife's fine. Kids are retarded.'

DAVID BECKHAM TO THE LINESMAN

David Beckham, in his early Real Madrid days, dropped a clanger, calling a linesman a 'hijo de puta', or 'son of a whore'. He was red carded and said: 'I didn't realise what I had said was that bad. I had heard a few of my team-mates say the same before me.'

ARSÈNE WENGER TO ALEX FERGUSON

Arsène Wenger responded to Alex Ferguson's claims that he had the best team in the Premier League in 2002 by saying: 'Everyone thinks they have the prettiest wife at home.'

GIOVANNI TRAPATTONI TO PAOLO DI CANIO

Giovanni Trapattoni, former manager of Italy, responded honestly to questions over whether he would select Paolo Di Canio for his 2004 World Cup squad: 'Only if there's an outbreak of bubonic plague.'

ROY KEANE TO MICK MCCARTHY

Roy Keane's alleged comments about Republic of Ireland manager Mick McCarthy were to the point. He is said to have claimed: 'You were a crap player, you are a crap manager. The only reason I have any dealings with you is that somehow you are manager of my country and you're not even Irish, you English ****. You can stick it up your bollocks.' Keane played no part in the 2002 World Cup.

JOHN MCENROE TO WIMBLEDON SPECTATOR

John McEnroe was famous for his loud mouth during matches and one time it overflowed onto the crowd with him screaming: 'What problems do you have, apart from being blind, unemployed and a moron?'

'And this is Gregoriava from Bulgaria. I saw her snatch this morning and it was amazing!'

Pat Glenn,
weightlifting commentator

SECRET TO SUCCESS

If sport was plain sailing, everybody would be chancing their arm at it. Some sports stars, though, rely on certain methods to ensure that they deliver the goods:

ANDY CARROLL

The West Ham striker was going through a torrid time at former club Liverpool, only to see the goals flow again with a winner at the death against Blackburn, then another late strike to sink rivals Everton in an FA Cup semi-final at Wembley. Team-mate Martin Kelly revealed that Carroll's secret was down to new hair gel that he borrowed from Jordan Henderson.

WAYNE ROONEY

There's a great deal more to Wazza than meets the eye. The England striker told ESPN that his secret was his powerful imagination. He lays back on the evening before a game, relaxes and simply visualises scoring goals for fun. This is not a recent trick either, the Manchester United legend having done it from his youth days at Everton. He said, 'You're trying to put yourself in that moment and trying to prepare yourself, to have a memory before the game. I don't know if you'd call it visualising or dreaming, but I've always done it, my whole life.'

PAPISS CISSÉ

The Newcastle United striker has revealed that the key to his goal gluts up on Tyneside has been curried goat made by the Magpies' chef Liz. The Senegalese international told the *Telegraph*, '[Newcastle have added] a Senegalese dish called Yassa [to the canteen menu], which I love. I can't cook it, but the chef at the club, Liz, does a really great job. It's fantastic. It is another example of how the club has made me feel so welcome and I appreciate it very much.'

Here's Zara after losing a bet

ZARA PHILLIPS

BORN: 15 May 1981, Paddington, London
CAREER HIGHLIGHTS: World gold, Olympic silver + BBC Sports
Personality of the Year

1) Zara had a pretty decent leg-up in life after being born to Princess
Anne and Captain Mark Phillips. The Queen's second eldest
grandchild, she qualified as a physiotherapist at Exeter University
before starting her equestrian career with second at 2003's Burghley
Horse Trials.
2) Phillips, who holds no royal title, soon picked up a string of
medals at the European and World Championships only to miss the
2004 and 2008 Olympics due to an injury to her horse Toytown.
She made up for it by winning silver in team eventing at the London
2012 Games.
3) Husband Mike Tindall has claimed Zara has set her sights on
winning gold at the 2016 Rio Olympics. He said, 'Her horse, High
Kingdom, has still got a good seven or eight years left in him.'
Reports that the horse is being wrapped in cotton wool until the
Games are hazy.
4) Zara's infamous £500,000 horse box comes complete with
granite-top kitchen and double bed. She's regularly seen driving the
26-tonne 'super-lorry', which has room for six horses and six human
companions. No word as of yet whether it can fit in the rest of the
Royal Family.

DID YOU KNOW: The happy couple watched the PDC Darts final
from the VIP area in 2012. Tindall made Zara laugh by donning a
beard, sunglasses and trilby hat before holding up a '180' sign. She
may've just been happy he'd covered his Sloth from Goonies face.

RECOVERY METHOD

Come on, fess up, we've all used some outlandish method to try and get over a niggle when we've fallen on our backside playing sport. What unusual recovery methods do the pros resort to after getting hobbled?

RAYMOND VAN BARNEVELD

'Barney' has delighted darts crowds all over the world with his unique brand of oche genius. The Dutchman, though, came to regret one attempt to recover his game during a rare slump in form. The five-time world champion employed hypnotist Sean Casey-Poole to give him a psychological edge ahead of a 2011 PDC World Championship match with bricklayer James Richardson, who was a massive 1,500–1 outsider for the tournament. Van Barneveld started off like a train thanks to a clinical 180, but soon slumped to a 3–0 defeat in just 37 minutes. After the defeat Casey-Poole tweeted, 'Devastated! Don't know what else to say!'

VITALI KLITSCHKO

'Dr Ironfist' bossed the world heavyweight division for a significant chunk of time after Lennox Lewis defeated him to end his own glittering career. The Ukrainian went nine years undefeated to retain his WBC strap before bowing out in 2012 against German Manuel Charr to start a career in politics. Klitschko once revealed that he used his son Max's wet nappies to stop his fists from swelling up in 2008 after administering a battering to 'The Nigerian Nightmare' aka Samuel Peter in Berlin. He said: 'Baby wee is good because it's pure, doesn't contain toxins and doesn't smell. The nappies hold the liquid and the swelling stays down.'

ROMELU LUKAKU

The burly Belgian has bullied defences for a few years in the Premier League with Chelsea and Everton as well as on the international stage for Belgium. Nevertheless, one recent injury almost got the better of him. His battering ram of a knee managed to clash with the poor head of Tottenham goalkeeper Hugo Lloris when the Toffees played against the Lilywhites. Lukaku posted an Instagram photo of him laid up with a bag of frozen vegetables, captioned: 'Hopefully I'll be better by tomorrow.' Unbelievably, French captain Lloris managed to carry on after the sickening connection despite being knocked out cold by the incident.

HOW TO

BECOME THE WORLD HEAVYWEIGHT BOXING CHAMPION

Boxing continues to hold a spell over legions of fans around the world. There's still nothing more primeval than watching two people bash the bejesus out of each other. After a dodgy era for the heavyweights, they are now king again, so see what it takes to pull on the biggest belt of all:

Leave prison and look for your closest gym.

Snarl and threaten to punch your opponent so hard even his ancestors will feel it – in a delightfully cute, girlish lisp.

Spar with an up-and-coming talent until your nose is shaped like a butternut squash.

Abuse, ridicule and insult your opponent at the press conference despite the fact you can barely move for crap in your pants.

Posture and enter the ring to pumping house music after your manager points out your favourite song '2 Become 1' isn't appropriate.

Cuddle a fat man for 12 three-minute rounds and call it a 'fight'.

Buy a watch more expensive than a house for everyone you meet.

The ECB management were so concerned about Kevin
getting up to antics on tour they kept an extra close eye on him

KEVIN PIETERSEN

BORN: 27 June 1980, Pietermaritzburg, Natal, South Africa
PLAYER: Nottinghamshire, Hampshire, Royal Challengers
Bangalore, Surrey, Deccan Chargers, Delhi Daredevils, Sunrisers
Hyderabad and England

1) Much like others in this book, KP's playing heroics and off-pitch antics could fill a whole tome by themselves. Pietersen, born
to an English mother, learnt his all-round trade in South Africa
before the dearly departed Clive Rice invited him over to play for
Nottinghamshire.

2) Pietersen soon made his mark with a string of centuries before
a move to Hampshire under fellow tabloid fodder Shane Warne
saw him earn his Test début against Australia in 2005. KP helped
Michael Vaughan's side put the Aussies to the sword in a famous
Ashes series win.

3) The flamboyant batsman continued to impress on the international
stage, his marriage to Liberty X singer Jessica Taylor adding fuel to
the media fire. Sadly, Pietersen's alledgedly rampant ego soon caused
friction in the England camp alongside his Indian Premier League
antics.

4) Former lover Gemma Hayley once claimed Pietersen was a selfish
lover. She revealed, 'Everything was centred around his own enjoyment.
He didn't care whether I was satisfied or not.' Thank your lucky stars he
didn't try one of his trademark switch hits in bed, Gemma.

DID YOU KNOW: As a child, Pietersen once put a chicken's head in
his mouth. He claimed, 'It was feathery and weird. Not the kind of
chicken I like.' What, as opposed to a smooth, boring chicken, KP?

HOW TO

PLAY LIKE A PREMIER LEAGUE FOOTBALLER

For many kids, growing up to be a Premier League footballer tops the wish list of dream jobs. Some possess the natural skill and are picked up immediately, while others journey there by the scenic route of the lower leagues. Here's how it's done properly:

Leave school when you're four and sign a 25-grand-a-week contract with an academy.

Score a goal and run to celebrate with the fans who were calling you a useless knobhead only 30 seconds earlier.

Write a statement of loyalty to your club on the back of your latest transfer request.

Put your hands on your head in wide-eyed astonishment for getting booked when you kicked an opponent's tits off.

Score once in 50 games – demand a pay rise.

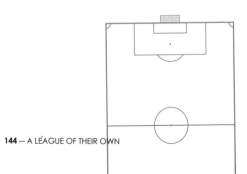

Go to matches wearing headphones so large you wouldn't notice if an aeroplane crash landed in the seat next to you on the bus.

SHORTEST DÉBUT

There is nothing like a rapid red card to make a sports star want the ground to swallow them whole. Check out these short débuts when the ref had to act:

LIONEL MESSI

The Barcelona wizard has enjoyed a tremendous career for the Spanish giants; however, it's not always been a bed of roses at international level. Itching to make a big impression on his début for Argentina, 18-year-old Messi managed to get sent off after just 44 seconds when he came on as a substitute against Hungary in 2005. The tears flowed in the dressing room according to team-mate Hernan Crespo, while Messi himself said, 'It wasn't the way I dreamed it would be. I passed him [Vilmos Vanczak] and he just grabbed me. I wanted to free myself so I could carry on and the referee judged that I had elbowed him. I was really disappointed as I had a lot of minutes left still to play, but what happened, happened.' Thankfully he only had to wait a few weeks for a full début redemption in a World Cup qualifier against Paraguay. He said: 'This is a re-début. The first one was a bit short.'

JOE COLE

Much like Messi, young Joe was set for big things from a very early age-coming through the ranks at West Ham alongside the likes of Rio Ferdinand. After impressive spells for the Hammers and Chelsea, together with England starts, Cole moved to Liverpool hoping to keep his magical run going. Sadly, the attacking midfielder was sent for an early bath by the ref in his Reds début against Arsenal with his straight red card for a foul on fellow debutant Laurent Koscielny coming in first-half injury time. Incredibly, Liverpool took the lead through David Ngog only for the Gunners to rescue a point through a last-minute own goal by Pepe Reina, while Koscielny also saw red. Boss Roy Hodgson said, 'He is devastated – his début, fantastic atmosphere, so desperate to do well. He was not playing at the top of his game.'

JONATHAN WOODGATE

Woodgate has not been the luckiest of footballers when it comes to injury, and when he has played at the top level he has suffered cruelly at the hand of fate. After sealing a bizarre move to Real Madrid in the summer of 2004, Woodgate spent the first year on the sidelines. Pumped up for his long-awaited full début in September 2005, Woody scored a spectacular own goal against Athletic Bilbao then got himself sent off for two bookable offences in the 65th minute. Voted worst signing of the twenty-first century by Spanish daily *Marca*, Woodgate was even quoted as saying after the game, 'F**k me, what a début!'

Here's Paula having some pre-race spaghetti

PAULA RADCLIFFE

BORN: 17 December 1973, Davenham, England
CAREER HIGHLIGHTS: World, European and Commonwealth gold
+ marathon world record

1) A phenomenal cross-country performer in her youth, Radcliffe
won gold at the World juniors in 1992 before winning the senior race
in 2001 and 2002. On the track, she eventually broke through into
stardom with gold at the 2002 European and Commonwealth meets.
2) She scooped BBC Sports Personality of the Year in 2002 and broke
the marathon world record twice with her time at the 2003 London
Marathon still standing. Radcliffe peaked with gold at the 2005 World
Championships after suffering Olympic heartache at Athens 2004.
3) Paula was caught short during the 2005 London Marathon and
took a public toilet break. She went on to win the race and declared
afterwards, 'I want to apologise to the nation.' Copycat events in school
playgrounds across the country did not go down well with teachers.
4) At the 2001 Worlds, Radcliffe held a sign saying 'EPO cheats out!'
as a protest against the reinstatement of Russian Olga Yegorova who
had tested positive for EPO. Radcliffe knew Olga was on drugs because
Lindsay Lohan was chasing her trying to ask who her dealer was.

DID YOU KNOW: Radcliffe is a famous chocoholic. Her obsession was
so bad at one stage that she used to hide chocolate bars under her bed
to avoid a ticking off from her husband, Gary Lough. Gary was scared
of monsters, so Paula managed to get away with it for years.

BEST EVER

FOOTBALLERS' NICKNAMES

Jason McAteer
'Trigger'

Jonathan Woodgate
'Village'

Tony Adams
'Donkey'

César Azpilicueta
'Dave'

Ray Parlour
'The Romford Pelé'

David James
'Calamity James'

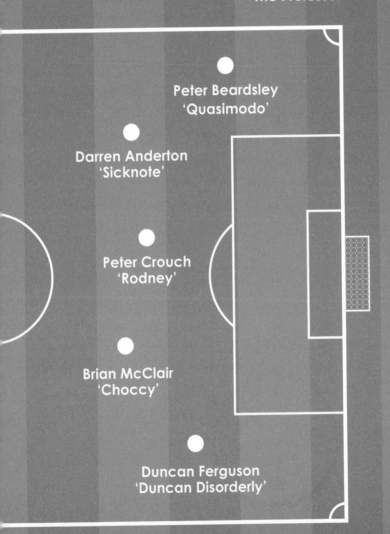

Everybody loves a nickname, whether it's the school playground, joshing around at work or going hell for leather as an amateur athlete. Just like chants, sporting nicknames give professionals and fans alike a chance to poke fun or mercilessly take the piss, so wallow in these beauties:

MANAGER   Arsène Wenger
– 'The Professor'

Peter Beardsley
'Quasimodo'

Darren Anderton
'Sicknote'

Peter Crouch
'Rodney'

Brian McClair
'Choccy'

Duncan Ferguson
'Duncan Disorderly'

Sport is not solely a land of bulked-up athletes and giants; there is the occasional short stop that finds their way into the pro ranks. Here's three of the best vertically challenged:

ÉLTON JOSÉ XAVIER GOMES

Brazilian attacking midfielder Gomes holds the distinction of being the tiniest male footballer at just 159cm (5ft 2in). The popular Afro-topped wizard plays for Al-Fateh in Saudi Arabia where he regularly dribbles through the legs of taller players. OK, slight exaggeration.

KRUGER VAN WYK

Kiwi wicketkeeper-batsman van Wyk pouches the leather at an astonishing 145cm (4ft 9in). Sadly for the South African-born player, his path into the team was barred by Mark Boucher, forcing his move to New Zealand. He made his Test début in 2012 against South Africa.

MUGGSY BOGUES

Tyrone 'Muggsy' Bogues is the shortest player in NBA history, standing at a teeny 160cm (5ft 3in). The waspish point guard ran rings around the giants of the hardcourt for 14 seasons but, despite a 44-inch vertical leap, his hands were too small to dunk one-handed. Bless.

'WE'RE GOING TO TURN THIS TEAM AROUND 360 DEGREES.'

JASON KIDD, BASKETBALL COACH
AND FORMER PLAYER

Here's Harry telling Luka Modrić what
he thinks of his move to Madrid

HARRY REDKNAPP

BORN: 2 March 1947, Poplar, London, England
PLAYER: West Ham, Bournemouth, Brentford and Seattle Sounders
MANAGER: Bournemouth, West Ham, Portsmouth, Southampton, Tottenham Hotspur and QPR

1) After learning his trade in the Tottenham youth ranks, West Ham snapped up the teenage midfielder and he made his first-téam debut in the 1965–66 season. He went on to play 149 times for the Hammers alongside Bobby Moore et al. before dropping down to Bournemouth.

2) Four ropey seasons on the south coast were followed by a stint as player-coach at Seattle Sounders. He became manager of Bournemouth in 1983, sparking a love affair with the touchline and journalist microphones that has since taken in five further top-flight clubs, with most success coming during his time at Tottenham.

3) Harry wakes up at 5am everyday to feed the birds in his garden. He revealed: 'We have about 30 and I can easily spend 80 quid on bird food a fortnight in the pet shop.' No doubt 'Arry haggled with the shopkeeper for hours about getting it on loan before closing the deal.

4) Redknapp famously got hoodwinked by Romanian international Florin Raducioiu, one of his biggest ever flop signings and there's been a few. The former Espanyol striker was seen out shopping in Harvey Nichols instead of playing an important Coca-Cola Cup game.

DID YOU KNOW: Incredibly, Redknapp was conned for three years by a fake jockey that he bankrolled for a series of free horse-racing tips. You'd have thought Harry would've realised the man was a fake jockey given that he was 6ft 4in and 16 stone.

ANCESTORS

You can hardly get through the day without a celebrity exploring their past on TV with a hanky close to hand. Here are some sports stars who have stars lurking in their family tree:

SVEN-GÖRAN ERIKSSON
The controversial former England boss's ancestry has been traced back to Field-Marshal Montgomery, who is descended from seventeenth-century battler William Sinclair of Saba.

WAYNE ROONEY
Legendary pugilist 'Ruby' Bob Fitzsimmons is linked with the current England striker through ancestral roots going back to his grandmother.

MATTHEW PINSENT
Four-time Olympic rowing champion and BBC TV presenter Pinsent is related to King Henry VIII, Edward I, William the Conqueror, Adam and Eve and therefore God.

'Ballesteros felt much better today after a 69 yesterday.'

Steve Ryder covering the Masters

Here's Dennis sharing a joke with a good mate ...

... and by the way that's not Michael McIntyre

DENNIS RODMAN

BORN: 13 May 1961, Trenton, New Jersey, USA
PLAYER: Detroit Pistons, San Antonio Spurs, Chicago Bulls, L.A. Lakers, Dallas Mavericks and Brighton Bears

1) Rodman started out his rollercoaster career as a small forward before moving into the power forward slot where he went on to shackle opposition offences for two decades. After being drafted by the Pistons, he helped Detroit to two NBA titles in a golden era for the city.
2) He then pitched up at San Antonio where his colourful, bombastic personality was at odds with the Spurs set-up, Chicago giving him a way out and three further titles. He was honoured as NBA Defensive Player of the Year and All-Star twice before retiring in 2006.
3) The New Jersey native was just as well known for his high-profile romantic liaisons with the likes of Madonna and marriage to Carmen Electra. Rodman claimed Madge was 'a control freak' for trying to get him to impregnate her and that Electra was the better lover of the two.
4) Rodman hit the headlines in 2014 for playing in a North Korea game to celebrate Kim Jong-un's birthday. He defended the trip in a CNN interview, saying it was 'a great idea for the world'. Yeah, just like nuclear weapons, human rights abuse and Dapper Laughs.

DID YOU KNOW: 'The Worm', as Rodman was nicknamed, wore a wedding dress to promote his 1996 autobiography *Bad as I Wanna Be* and said Michael Jordan would look as good in a gown. He also revealed he was marrying himself, so take it all with a pinch of salt.

BEST EVER

FOOTBALLERS' NICKNAMES #2

Fitz Hall
'One Size'

Roberto Baggio
'The Divine Ponytail'

Robbie Fowler
'God'

Peter Schmeichel
'The Great Dane'

Stuart Pearce
'Psycho'

David Beckham
'Golden Balls'

MANAGER José Mourinho
'The Special One'

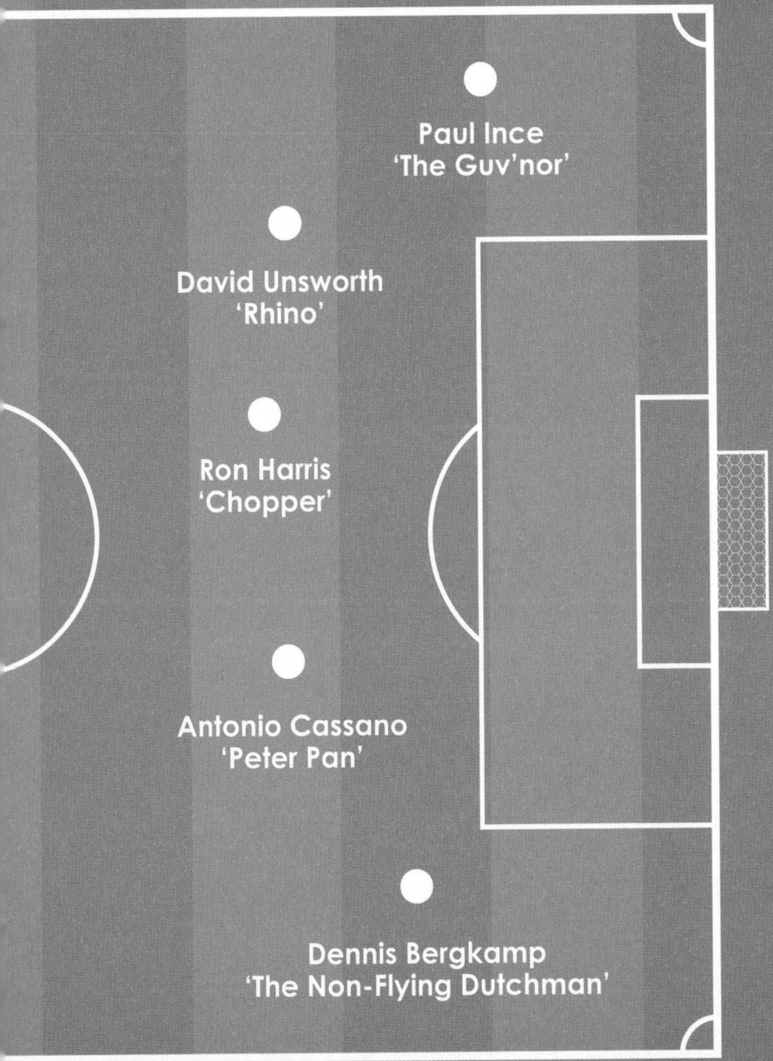

Paul Ince
'The Guv'nor'

David Unsworth
'Rhino'

Ron Harris
'Chopper'

Antonio Cassano
'Peter Pan'

Dennis Bergkamp
'The Non-Flying Dutchman'

Here's Cristiano about to be mistaken for the Brazilian Ronaldo

CRISTIANO RONALDO

BORN: 5 February 1985, Funchal, Madeira, Portugal
PLAYER: Sporting Lisbon, Manchester United, Real Madrid and Portugal

1) Ronaldo had barely begun to make his name in the sporting history books before Fergie plucked him from Portugal to become an Old Trafford player after the wing wizard played a pivotal part in the Portuguese side putting the visitors to the sword in a Lisbon friendly.

2) The confident youngster soon became a United legend in the making with a string of preposterously good displays that underpinned annual trophy sweeps at home and abroad, with the cheeky chappy eventually finishing with 84 goals in 196 games for the club.

3) Even though his national side could never reach the meteoric heights he has achieved personally in winning three Ballons d'Or, his Real Madrid career has seen an avalanche of goals, Spanish titles and the famous 2014 Champions League win in La Decima season. ('La Decima' means 'tenth' in Spanish and refers to Madrid's record-breaking tenth European Cup/Champions League win.)

4) Ronaldo believes Manc legends Oasis are a better band than The Beatles. Oasis had that one arrogant guy who thought he was better than the rest of the group – so God knows why Ronaldo can relate them.

DID YOU KNOW: The Portuguese superstar picked up a love of bingo during his United days and it also helped him learn English words and phrases. Reports suggested he cheekily used to look over at Wayne Rooney when 60 was called with 'Grandma's getting frisky'.

TEAM BONDING

We all need a spot of team bonding every now and then to boost morale, whether it's a night on the razzle or building a ropey raft. Here's a few belters from the world of sport:

ENGLAND

Boss Roy Hodgson took the squad to a shooting range at Euro 2012 to try and build team spirit ahead of their Italy match. They travelled to an indoor range near Krakow after a round of golf and blasted live ammunition from AK-47 assault rifles and Magnum pistols. Players like Andy Carroll, Danny Welbeck, Ashley Young and Alex Oxlade-Chamberlain zeroed in on the targets, with Carroll posing for team-mates with a black assault rifle in each hand.

MANCHESTER UNITED

Ahead of the 2012/13 season, Sir Alex Ferguson took his squad to Durban in South Africa and visited a tribe after stopping off at the PheZulu Safari Park. The United players spent time with tribal drums and then dressed up as African tribal warriors for the press corps.

NEWCASTLE UNITED

Unlike Manchester United, the Magpies kept things simpler when it came to team bonding. They held *Come Dine with Me* evenings in 2012 according to Mike Williamson. He gave James Perch's baked potatoes zip out of ten and claimed Shola Amoebi 'leaves it all to his missus'.

Here's 'Fat Ronaldo' enjoying his retirement …

… or, as Razor Ruddock calls him, 'Thin Ronaldo'

RONALDO

BORN: 18 September 1976, Rio de Janeiro, Brazil
PLAYER: Cruzeiro, PSV, Barcelona, Inter Milan, Real Madrid, AC
Milan, Corinthians and Brazil

1) Ronaldo catapulted himself into Brazilian hearts and minds aged
17 when he hammered five goals in a single game for Cruzeiro against
Bahia. He soon earned a Brazil call-up for the 1994 World Cup and,
even though he didn't play, PSV Eindhoven brought him to Europe.
2) The prolific striker was in no mood to stop his goal plundering: 54
goals in 58 games in Holland were followed by brilliant displays at a
host of top European clubs. It was his goals for winners Brazil in the
2002 World Cup that truly cemented his status as a football legend.
3) Ronaldo once confessed on Brazilian TV, 'I have this recurring
dream where I'm going to the bathroom to pass water. The next thing
I know, my bed is all wet.' It's called pissing your bed, Ronny. At least
it wasn't alcohol influenced, like most English players in the 1970s.
4) The man named 'Il Fenomeno' has proved a phenomenon with the
ladies, racking up three weddings and four children by three women.
He later had a vasectomy, announcing he was 'closing the factory'.
Overworked Brazilian DNA lab technicians breathed a sigh of relief.

DID YOU KNOW: Ronaldo admitted to weeping in 2008 after
discovering that three shady ladies he took back to his hotel room
were transvestites. The Brazilian exhorted, 'This will stain my life
forever.' Well it's certainly something Vanish or Cilit Bang will fail to
remove.

'IT'S LAP 26 OF 58, WHICH UNLESS I'M VERY MUCH MISTAKEN IS HALF WAY.'

MURRAY WALKER

HOW TO

SURVIVE AS A COUNTY CRICKETER

Glamorous is not a word that you would readily associate with the poor souls who have to trudge out for the poorly attended and only adequately catered county cricket matches. So what does it take to make the grade?

Get your parents to mark out a 22-yard wicket and 450-foot boundary in your garden so you can train.

Practise hard and use your God-given talent to deal with the pressure of entertaining crowds of up to seven people.

Keep as quiet as possible when fielding – the fans get really annoyed if you wake them.

Hope the six you've hit is up there in terms of cricketing excitement with the *You've Been Framed* clip when a dad got hit in the spuds by his son's follow-through.

Because you're a professional athlete only eat isotonic, health-giving quiche and bacon sandwiches during the two full meals you have during the game.

Consider the man from Pretoria who only speaks Afrikaans to be the best English cricketer you've played with.

Here is Hodgson saying, 'Wayne, if you need a wee, stop drinking'

WAYNE ROONEY

BORN: 24 October 1985, Liverpool, England
PLAYER: Everton, Manchester United and England

1) Wazza grew up an ardent Toffees fan, so was particularly made up when they offered to take him on aged just nine. Within six years he was plundering goals left, right and centre for the U19s and banged in eight goals in eight games during the 2002 FA Youth Cup final run.

2) He laid on an assist on his senior Everton début against Spurs later that year and handed in a transfer request two years on from that after scoring 15 goals in 67 games. Manchester United duly took him on, where he became a prolific goal scorer and England regular up front.

3) Rooney bonded with legend Elton John over hair-transplant stories after meeting backstage on a trip to Las Vegas. Although if there's one person you should take it with a pinch of salt if they tell you your hair looks good, it's Elton John.

4) Wayne's volatile temper included a tendency to smash mobile phones, according to Rio Ferdinand. Rio said, 'He seemed to fly into a rage about the smallest things and went through mobile phones like they were sweets.' Well, we all get fed up with PPI calls, but that's mad.

DID YOU KNOW: Wazza saved wife Coleen from drowning on their first foreign holiday in 2003. He swam out to rescue her with the current so strong that it had pulled Coleen's bikini bottoms off. Writers for the next *Carry On* film didn't have to look far for their next plot.

TEENAGE KICKS

Teenagers get up to all sorts of mischief. After all it's a God-given right to knock about acting like a goon before responsibility hits. What did our sports stars do in their formative years?

ZLATAN IBRAHIMOVIĆ

The sumptuous Swede has gifted the football world with a phalanx of galactic goals during the course of his trophy-laden career. He has racked up goal-scoring records and league titles at an astonishing rate in Holland, Italy, Spain and France, but how did it all begin for the son of a Bosnian father and Croatian mother? Well, the Swede revealed in his autobiography that he used to steal bikes in his teenage years. Not content with nicking bog-standard bikes, 'Ibracadabra' pedalled off with a postman's bike once and also the coach's bike at his first club. The mischievous striker recalled with glee, 'I picked the locks. I got to be an expert at it. Boom, boom – and the bike was mine. I was the bicycle thief. That was my first thing.'

WLADIMIR KLITSCHKO

Youngest of the two heavyweight boxing world champion brothers, Wladimir has revealed a quite staggering teenage kick. The Ukrainian grew up on a military base with older brother Vitali and they used to get up to no end of mischief. 'Dr Steelhammer' once found live ammunition and some grenades. Any normal kid would have left it well alone or given it to an adult to deal with, but not Wlad. Along with Vitali, they chucked them into a fire! He claimed, 'It made a lot of noise, it was fun.' They also brought an anti-tank mine home with them and tried to hide it under their parents' beds. Needless to say, it didn't go down too well.

EDEN HAZARD

Chelsea's midfield maestro always wanted to play football, no matter what. Lille, Blues and Belgium fans must be grateful that teenage forays into private land didn't end with a spell in juvie. The diminutive Eden used to climb over a barrier to play on the local club's training pitches with his brother in order to curl in trademark free kicks and penalties. They were once caught by the club's president and facing retribution, only to leg it away in the nick of time.

Here's Maria finding out Jack Whitehall has got hold of her phone number

MARIA SHARAPOVA

BORN: 19 April 1987, Nyagan, Russia
CAREER HIGHLIGHTS: Five-time Grand Slam champion and
Olympic silver medallist

1) Maria was given her first tennis racquet at four and attended
a tennis clinic aged just six run by Martina Navratilova, who
recommended she train at Nick Bollettieri's famous academy in
Florida. Her father Yuri saved up to take her over and worked hard
to pay her way through it.

2) The blonde bombshell reached two junior Grand Slam finals,
including the 2002 Wimbledon, before stunning Serena Williams
as a 17-year-old to win the senior title in 2004. She's since
completed the career Grand Slam with victories at the Australian,
French and US Opens.

3) Sharapova became the first woman to carry the Russian flag at the
Olympics. She said, 'I am so honoured as it will be my first Olympics
in my career.' It's a shame Vladimir Putin didn't try to hijack another
big moment as he'd look even more hilarious in a blonde wig.

4) The Russian has developed her own brand of candy and
sweets called Sugarpova. She sells a wide range around the world,
including Sporty, Flirty and Splashy; however, her Grunty line
didn't go down too well in the Wimbledon area after her annual
decibel carnage at SW19.

DID YOU KNOW: Maria collects stamps in her spare time. She said,
'The coolest thing is finding an excuse to go to the post office and do
something different.' Rumours that Serena Williams often train-spots
at Clapham Junction to unwind during Wimbledon are now rife.

BEST EVER

★ ★ ★ ★ ★ ★ ★ ★ ★

BOXING NICKNAMES

MIKE TYSON
'IRON MIKE'

VS

MUHAMMAD ALI
'THE GREATEST'

ERIC ESCHE 'BUTTERBEAN'

★  **VS** ★

JAMES 'BONECRUSHER' SMITH

★ ★ ★ ★ ★ ★ ★ ★ ★

JAMES
'LIGHTS OUT'
TONEY

RAY
'BOOM BOOM'
MANCINI

'PRINCE'
NASEEM HAMED

JUAN
'THE HISPANIC CAUSIN' PANIC'
LAZCANO

MIKE
'BODYSNATCHER'
MCCALLUM

OSCAR DE LA
HOYA
'GOLDENBOY'

In fairness to Uruguay, they did introduce this new anti-biting kit

LUIS SUÁREZ

BORN: 24 January 1987, Salto, Uruguay
PLAYER: Nacional, Groningen, Ajax, Liverpool, Barcelona and
Uruguay

1) Suárez came through an unconventional route to the top, a brief
spell at Nacional in his home country of Uruguay followed by a move
to unfashionable Groningen in Holland aged just 19. After just one
season, Dutch giants Ajax sealed a controversial move for the striker.
2) The buck-toothed goal poacher plundered 81 goals in just
110 appearances for Ajax and several more for Uruguay before
a £22.8 million move to Liverpool in the 2011 January transfer
window. Suárez's astonishing goals alone nearly helped the Reds
win the title in 2014.
3) In echoes of Cantona, Suarez has hit the front pages as prolifically
as he has the back. His bare-faced handling of the ball to deny Ghana
a famous quarter-final victory at the 2010 World Cup cemented his
global status as a pantomime villain that he's added to since.
4) Suárez can count bad-boy boxer Mike Tyson amongst his Twitter
followers. Both have been involved in high-profile biting incidents;
however, Suárez will have to raise his game to eclipse the world
heavyweight champion, who is still digesting Evander Holyfield's ear.

DID YOU KNOW: The Barcelona forward revealed that before joining
the Spanish giants he'd previously got into Camp Nou through an
open gate to have a picture taken with his girlfriend – the caretaker
had left it open whilst he was bite-proofing it ready for Luis's arrival.

UNLIKELY FRIENDSHIP

*When celebrities collide in the world of sport and entertainment it can lead to
some highly amusing pairings, which give the tabloids acres of copy. Here are
some of our favourites:*

STEVEN GERRARD

In one of the most ridiculous pairings in celebrity history, the former
England captain and *Sex and the City* star Kim Cattrall are best
buddies. The Hollywood actress is Merseyside born and has spent
several years working in England since her hit show finished. In 2010
Kim was a guest of Steven's in his private box. She said, 'I did go to
Anfield when I was there, and Steven and his lovely wife came to see
me in the play [*Antony and Cleopatra*].'

FLOYD MAYWEATHER, JR

The ring entrances of 'Pretty Boy' have become weirder and
weirder the nearer that the undefeated king has got to retirement.
Not content with inviting the Burger King mascot into the ring with
him ahead of the Manny Pacquiao megafight, Floyd brought pop
sensation Justin Bieber along too. The Canadian has apparently been
getting boxing lessons from the champ.

THEO WALCOTT

England wing wizard Walcott has his very own wizard to call upon when he is kicking back away from the football pitch. The Arsenal player has revealed that Harry Potter himself, Daniel Radcliffe, is a pal. He said, 'I get on well with Daniel Radcliffe from Harry Potter. He's the kind of friend that I can invite around to my house for a meal and hang out with. He's a good lad. There are obviously quite a few footballers' numbers in my phone, too!'

Mike's quite a hero nowadays. If he ever spots someone
in trouble in a river he sends his pet in to help ...

... you'd see the tiger and get out of the water. Then
you'd see Mike Tyson and jump back in.

MIKE TYSON

BORN: 30 June 1966, Brooklyn, New York, USA
CAREER HIGHLIGHTS: Heavyweight world champion with 44 KOs in 58 fights

1) Tyson had a difficult childhood in Brooklyn, not helped by his pronounced lisp and high-pitched voice. His saviour came in the form of legendary boxing manager and trainer Cus D'Amato, who took the firebrand under his wing and moulded him into a wrecking ball.
2) He cleaned up at the Junior Olympics as an amateur but, after missing out on a shot at the 1984 Olympics in Los Angeles, he turned pro in 1985. He racked up 27 wins in under 18 months before stopping Trevor Berbick to win the WBC world heavyweight title in 1986.
3) Iron Mike claimed he walked in on his ex-wife Robin Givens in bed with Brad Pitt. He refers to the Hollywood star as 'a broken down, bootleg version of Robert Redford'. Brad was not available for comment on what he refers to 'The Baddest Man on the Planet'.
4) Tyson claimed, 'I can sell out Madison Square Garden masturbating' – if he ever does and you're sitting near the front, we sincerely recommend buying a Seaworld-style poncho.

DID YOU KNOW: Mike did the voice-over for his character in the cartoon *Mike Tyson Mysteries.* His sidekick is a foul-mouthed pigeon and they solve crazy capers involving an author who also happens to be a werewolf. LSD is obviously popular in US writers' rooms.

HOW TO

WIN A GRAND PRIX

What does it take to win a Grand Prix as one of Formula 1's elite drivers?

It's simple – all you need are lightning-fast reflexes, nerves of steel, wealthy parents to buy you a go-kart, tactical awareness, a multi-million-pound vehicle and the backing of Europe's top car engineers and designers.

Don't wear ear defenders – that way you won't be able to hear your pop-star girlfriend's latest album.

'Do it for Britain' – by living in a European tax haven.

Overtake less often than an elderly woman on the way to the post office.

Obey orders from a 4ft-tall, white-haired billionaire in shades.

Drive to win! Unless it's your team-mate's turn to win – in which case, spin off into the advertising hoardings.

'*People say Ronnie O'Sullivan is the best thing in snooker since Tiger Woods.*'

Willie Thorne, former professional snooker player

Here is the moment Warnie was told that there was no
facial scrub available on his 12-hour flight

SHANE WARNE

BORN: 13 September 1969, Upper Ferntree Gully, Australia
PLAYER: Victoria, Hampshire, Rajasthan Royals, Melbourne Stars
and Australia

1) Believe it or not, Warnie was let go by Accrington Cricket Club in
1991 despite taking 73 wickets at 15.4 each. He returned to his native
Australia, buckled down and made his first-class début for Victoria en
route to a call-up for the third Test against India in 1992.
2) There will probably never be a better introduction to Ashes cricket
than Warne's first ball in the 1993 series in England. The ferocious leg
spinner managed to turn the ball sideways to dismiss flapping home
legend Mike Gatting in what was called the 'ball of the century'.
3) Warne's off-pitch behaviour as a peroxide blond rogue has been as
tabloid-worthy as his cricketing skills, while he was sent home from the
2003 World Cup after failing a drugs test. He said his mum gave him
the drugs – bloody hell, ours wouldn't even let us have Haribo.
4) Shane made quite the impression in the Indian Premier League
with his celebrity lifestyle, but found the food challenging. He now
claims 'to love chicken tikka masala'. Nothing like going all that way to
Asia to fall in love with a dish invented back in his adopted England.

DID YOU KNOW: During his relationship with actress Liz Hurley,
Warnie made a bizarre appearance at New York Fashion Week
alongside her and their pal Sarah Jessica Parker. The models turned
heads on the catwalk; sadly Shane couldn't after his latest cosmetic
procedure.

When we asked for a photo of Amy being dirty,
this wasn't what we hoped for

AMY WILLIAMS

BORN: 29 September 1982, Cambridge, England
CAREER HIGHLIGHTS: Gold medallist in the skeleton at the 2010 Winter Olympics

1) Williams propelled herself into the nation's hearts via the highly dangerous skeleton event in Vancouver. She began her career as a runner, but switched to the ice in a savvy career move that saw her become Britain's first female individual Winter Olympics gold medallist in 58 years.

2) Injuries soon put paid to the 2014 defence of her title, but a lucrative gig as *Ski Sunday* co-presenter alongside the Peter Pan of winter sports Martin Bell ensured that the public would still get their fill of the feisty competitor nicknamed 'Curly Wurly' because of her frizzy hair.

3) Williams went head-to-head with a Mini Cooper in Lillehammer during a 2011 episode of *Top Gear*. The tray tumbler was 1.31 seconds slower on her skeleton down the Olympic track than the flat-out car, which covered the same distance on a road interweaving the circuit.

4) The Cambridge native named her skeleton sled 'Arthur' as she wanted a decent English name 'that also said Grr'. We know it sounds a bit mad, but in fairness you'd have to be to hurtle down an ice slide at 80mph.

DID YOU KNOW: Amy was awarded an MBE in the 2010 Queen's Birthday Honours and was also made an honorary freeman of Bath the same year. She was only the fifth person since the Second World War to achieve this, after famous predecessors Winston Churchill and, erm, sprinter Jason Gardener.

UNUSUAL CREDIT

We find out pretty quickly what fuelled sporting victories in post-match interviews and it's usually pretty humdrum stuff, so revel in this selection of bizarre reasons behind triumphs:

GORAN IVANIŠEVIĆ

The charismatic Croatian credits his wonderful wildcard Wimbledon victory in 2001 to a routine that involved a famous kids' TV programme as inspiration. Every day, he began by watching *Teletubbies* and each night he ate dinner at the same table in the same restaurant, always ordering fish soup, lamb with potatoes and ice cream with chocolate sauce.

LIZZY YARNOLD

The 2014 Winter Olympic gold medallist from Sochi credits her rather unique preparation for giving her that decisive edge in the skeleton. She revealed, 'What does one do during the overnight gap between the two most important days of your life? Watch *Poirot*.'

DIEGO SIMEONE

Atlético Madrid's manager pinpointed the testicles of his players for helping them defeat Chelsea in the Champions League. The Argentinian said, 'I want to thank the mothers of these players because they gave birth to them with balls this big,' gesturing as if holding a football.

'Chemistry is a class you take in high school or college, where you figure out two plus two is ten, or something.'

DENNIS RODMAN

Here's Serena just wondering if her new hat meets Wimbledon kit restrictions

SERENA WILLIAMS

BORN: 26 September 1981, Saginaw, Michigan, USA
CAREER HIGHLIGHTS: 21 Grand Slam singles, 15 doubles + four
Olympic gold medals

1) The youngest of five daughters by mother Oracene, Serena grew
up home schooled with sister Venus as father Richard moulded
them into future Grand Slam champions. Incredibly, Serena's first
professional event was aged 14 in 1995 and her first tournament win
came in 1999.
2) After picking up Grand Slam doubles titles for fun with Venus and
male mixed doubles partners, Serena began to eclipse her sister in the
singles after winning her first at the 1999 US Open. She completed
the career Grand Slam with Australian Open victory in 2003.
3) Her SerenaFriday Twitter Q&As have unearthed some gems since
she started it, including the fact that she'd like to star in an action
movie and that her favourite *Avengers* character is Hulk or Thor. Film
fans would pay good money to see Serena take on Iron Man in the
next movie.
4) Serena dated rapper Common on and off for three years, then
switched her attention to Canadian TV star-turned-rapper Drake.
Both insist the relationship is platonic; however, the two artists
have exchanged insults via their songs, with Serena rumoured to
be the reason.

DID YOU KNOW: After Andy Murray suggested players should
entertain the crowd with karaoke in rain breaks, Serena backed him.
Murray picked REM's 'Losing My Religion' with Serena preferring
old Wimbledon favourite 'Straight Outta Compton' by NWA.

WORST FEATURE

It's an oft-told tale that sportsmen and women spend more time looking in the mirror than practising their skills, so it's a surprise to find some don't rate certain parts of their bodies:

ERIC CANTONA

When asked by the *Independent* whether he would change anything about himself, the Frenchman said: 'Nothing, I have nothing to change. I would change others around me. I see the world become so uniform. Everybody has to be the same. I like people who are different.'

USAIN BOLT

The Olympic king told the *Observer*, 'I am not proud of my toes. They are not very pretty. Other than my toes, I feel good about my body. My arms and my abs are particularly nice.'

MIKE TINDALL

Rugby World Cup winner Mike Tindall told the *Guardian*, 'I haven't straight teeth. I was a stubborn kid and refused when Mum and Dad tried to encourage me to get braces. I regret it now.'

"'You may as well put a cow in the middle of the pitch, walking. And then stop the game because there was a cow.'

JOSÉ MOURINHO ON NEWCASTLE UNITED'S TIME-WASTING TACTICS

HOW TO

WIN THE TOUR DE FRANCE

Anyone who believes cyclists haven't been on the wacky juice for decades needs their heads looking at. Despite that, the Tour de France quite rightly remains an iconic race. Here's how you can pull on le maillot jaune in true Gallic style:

After realising that the race is 3,000 miles, many of them over mountains, you'll need to be on some sort of drugs to even consider it.

Buy some of those shoes that clip into the pedals – they're cool.

Deny you've taken steroids despite going faster than a motorbike.

Remove the tassels from your handlebars and Hannah Montana spokey-dokeys – you're a professional.

Refuse to admit your coach is injecting you with steroids – even though her name is Dr Anna Bolic and you've got arms more muscular than Thor's legs.

Wear shorts that are tighter than your scrotum.

Get urine thrown at you by fans – but be grateful because you need a clean sample.

Here's Tiger auditioning a new caddy

TIGER WOODS

BORN: 30 December 1975, Cypress, California, USA
CAREER HIGHLIGHTS: 14 Majors + career slam of Masters, US
Open, Open and US PGA

1) Much like the Williams sisters, Tiger was a child prodigy driven by
a single-minded father. He smashed age records at every turn while he
also putted against Bob Hope on TV aged just two. He broke 70 on a
regulation golf course at 12 and won the US Amateur in 1994.
2) Tiger turned pro in 1996 with sponsorship deals from Nike and
Titleist in his back pocket. He won his first Major the following year at
the Masters, going on to challenge Jack Nicklaus as the greatest ever
player with a further 13 Majors before the wheels came off in 2009.
3) His former swing coach Hank Haney revealed Tiger considered
giving up golf and joining the Navy SEALs. He'd be brilliant in
Special Operations – provided the missions were either a tricky 13th
hole or breaking into a waitress's knickers.
4) Woods started wearing a pink Buddhism bracelet in March
2010 to offer him 'strength and protection' and remind him of the
principles of the faith that his mother followed. If reincarnation's
real, Tiger will come back as a dog on heat.

DID YOU KNOW: The billionaire golfer unwinds in classic Robinson
Crusoe style. The American revealed, 'I like to go spear-fishing.
Anything that has to do with water, I just absolutely love it.' His
favourite fishing spots are Alaska, Ireland and his local Hooters.

QUIZZES

ANSWERS ON PAGE 209

BOOZIEST

Sporting events are often best enjoyed with a cheeky pint or five, cases of vino or several jugs of Pimm's. There are some that have traditionally been known for drunken tomfoolery, while others have been rather more restrained. See if you can match up the pint output to the event.

World Snooker Championship, Crucible, Sheffield	**3.9 pints per person**
England v India Test, Lords	**0.49 pints per person**
England rugby game, Twickenham	**0.19 pints per person**
PDC World Darts Championship	**2.6 pints per person**
Royal Ascot	**0.53 pints per person**
Cheltenham Festival	**10 pints per person**
Wimbledon	**1.22 pints per person**
Welsh rugby game, Cardiff Millennium Stadium	**0.56 pints per person**

MUSIC

There have been classic songs released by football teams over the years, whether it's the local act of your own club or a rousing national anthem that makes the hair on the back of your neck stand up. Try and rank the singles by the number of weeks they were in the UK top 75.

Rank	Year	Team/Artist	Single	Chart peak
	1970	England World Cup squad	'Back Home'	1
	1994	Manchester United FA Cup squad	'Come On You Reds'	1
	1982	England World Cup squad	'This Time (We'll Get It Right)'	2
	1990	England World cup squad/New Order	'World in Motion'	1
	1981	Tottenham Hotspur FA Cup squad	'Ossie's Dream (Spurs Are on Their Way to Wembley)'	5
	1971	Arsenal first team squad	'Good Old Arsenal'	16
	1988	Liverpool	'Anfield Rap (Red Machine in Full Effect)'	3
	1985	Everton	'Here We Go'	14
	1996	Liverpool and Boot Room Boyz	'Pass & Move (It's the Liverpool Groove)'	4
	1990	Scottish World Cup squad	'Say It with Pride'	45
	1977	West Ham United FA Cup squad	'I'm Forever Blowing Bubbles'	31

THE SMARTEST

Believe it or not, there are some sports stars who haven't grown up in a bubble their whole lives and want to chow down on brain food outside of the gladiatorial arena – yes, even footballers. Have a go at matching the educational high points with our sporting nerds.

. . . .

Socrates	Law degree (University of Split)
Andrey Ashavin	Ten grade A GCSEs
Joey Barton	Gave an hour-long talk about philosophy and social media at the Oxford Union
Dennis Bergkamp	A GCSE in Latin
Slaven Bilić	Fashion design degree
Will Carling	Qualified doctor and PhD in philosophy
Clark Carlisle	Intern at NASA
Petr Cech	Started an environmental science degree but dropped out
Shaka Hislop	Economics degree (Durham University)
Michael Jordan	Psychology degree (Durham University)
Frank Lampard	Master's in sports management (Johan Cruyff Institute, Amsterdam)
Graeme Le Saux	Economics degree (University of Strasbourg)
Brian McClair	Cultural geography degree (University of North Carolina)
Simon Mignolet	Maths degree (Glasgow University)
Manuel Pellegrini	Law degree (Swansea University)
Andrew Strauss	Political science degree (University of Leuven)
Edwin van der Sar	Qualified civil engineer
Arsène Wenger	Law degree
Alun Wyn Jones	Mechanical engineering degree (Bath University)

SPORTS STARS' EMBARRASSING SECRETS

It's hard to keep anything schtum in this day and age, what with social media worming its way into our lives. As a result, we know pretty much all there is to know about our sports stars, so which secret belongs to which person?

Chris Ashton	incredibly clumsy
Steve Bruce	stood on Bill Clinton's foot
Mark Cavendish	former ballroom dancer
Carl Froch	smoked when he was younger
Lewis Hamilton	has a fruit skin phobia
Amie Khan	loves Desperate Housewives
Ledley King	read all the Harry Potter books at least five times
Andy Murray	quit karate after losing to the opposite sex
Greg Rutherford	scared of rats
Beth Tweddle	addicted to Fantasy Football
Serena Williams	hates it when marks appear on his white trainers

SPORTS STARS' HOBBIES

We've all got one thing that makes us exude calm outside of the rollercoaster called life – a hobby where you can kick back and take your mind off the big prize. Sports stars are no different, so try and see if you can match the person to the eclectic hobbies below.

• •

Daniel Agger	Magic
Fernando Alonso	Bingo
Manuel Alumnia	Drums
David Beckham	Star Wars films (owns an Imperial Storm Trooper outfit)
Darren Bent	Second World War books
Wayne Bridge	Winemaking
Petr Cech	Stamp collecting
Michael Essien	Yoga
Les Ferdinand	Rollerblading
Ryan Giggs	Raising pigeons
Shaq O'Neil	Wife carrying
Andrea Pirlo	Police work
Dennis Rodman	Monopoly
Cristiano Ronaldo	Invested £20,000 in a soft-core porn channel
Greg Rusedski	Tattoo artist
Maria Sharapova	Sleeping
Mike Tyson	Helicopter pilot
Shaun Wright-Phillips	Fencing (does it at Tom Cruise's house with Will Smith)

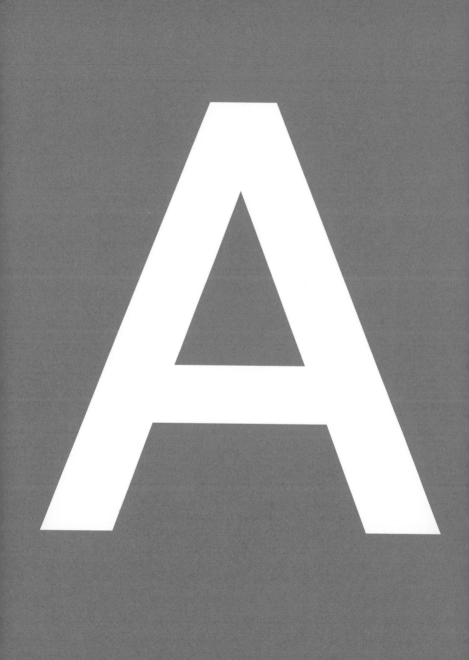

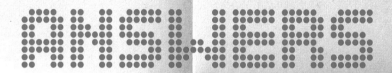

ANSWERS

BOOZIEST

PDC World Darts Championship

10 pints per person. 350,000 over 11 days. 31,818 per day. 35,000 aggregate attendance. Average 3,181 people a day.

England v India Test, Lords

2.6 pints per person. Attendance over the five-day series: 125,000. Total beers drunk over the course of the test: 325,642.

England rugby game, Twickenham

0.53 pints per person. 80,000 fans drank 44,000 pints.

World Snooker Championship, Crucible, Sheffield

0.49 pints per person. The final day had an attendance of 921, with 456 pints consumed.

Royal Ascot

0.56 pints per person. 160,000 pints drunk over five days, 32,000 per day. 284,196 total attendance, 56,839 per day.

Cheltenham Festival

3.9 pints per person. Total pints consumed: 199,469. Attendance 50,000.

Wimbledon

0.19 pints per person. 7,308 pints drank per day, 489,896 total. Average attendance 37,684 per day.

Welsh rugby game, Cardiff Millennium Stadium

1.22 pints per person. Total pints consumed: 199,469. Attendance 50,000.

MUSIC

Rank	Year	Team/Artist	Single	Chart peak	Chart peak
1st	1970	England World Cup squad	'Back Home'	1	17
2nd	1994	Manchester United FA Cup squad	'Come On You Reds'	1	16
3rd	1982	England World Cup squad	'This Time (We'll Get It Right)'	2	13
4th	1990	England World cup squad/New Order	'World in Motion'	1	12
5th	1981	Tottenham Hotspur FA Cup squad	'Ossie's Dream (Spurs Are on Their Way to Wembley)'	5	8
6th	1971	Arsenal first team squad	'Good Old Arsenal'	16	7
7th	1988	Liverpool	'Anfield Rap (Red Machine in Full Effect)'	3	6
8th	1985	Everton	'Here We Go'	14	5
9th	1996	Liverpool and Boot Room Boyz	'Pass & Move (It's the Liverpool Groove)'	4	5
10th	1990	Scottish World Cup squad	'Say It with Pride'	45	3
11th	1977	West Ham United FA Cup squad	'I'm Forever Blowing Bubbles'	31	2

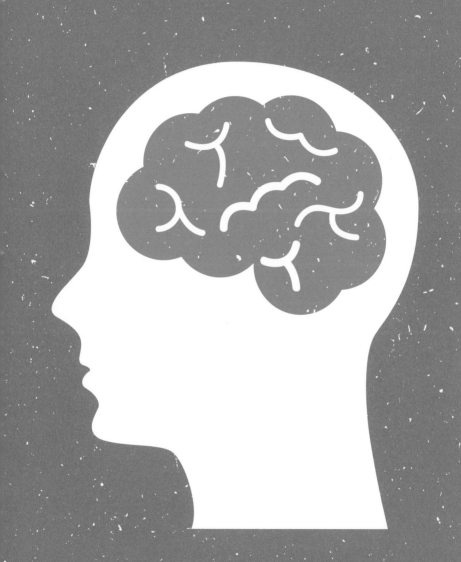

THE SMARTEST

Slaven Bilić	Law degree (University of Split)
Clark Carlisle	Ten grade A GCSEs
Joey Barton	Gave an hour-long talk about philosophy and social media at the Oxford Union
Frank Lampard	A GCSE in Latin
Andrey Ashavin	Fashion design degree
Socrates	Qualified doctor and PhD in philosophy
Shaka Hislop	Intern at NASA
Graeme Le Saux	Started an environmental science degree but dropped out
Andrew Strauss	Economics degree (Durham University)
Will Carling	Psychology degree (Durham University)
Edwin van der Sar	Master's in sports management (Johan Cruyff Institute, Amsterdam)
Arsène Wenger	Economics degree (University of Strasbourg)
Michael Jordan	Cultural geography degree (University of North Carolina)
Brian McClair	Maths degree (Glasgow University)
Alun Wyn Jones	Law degree (Swansea University)
Simon Mignolet	Political science degree (University of Leuven)
Manuel Pellegrini	Qualified civil engineer
Petr Cech	Law degree
Dennis Bergkamp	Mechanical engineering degree (Bath University)

SPORTS STARS' EMBARRASSING SECRETS

Steve Bruce smoked when he was younger

Mark Cavendish former ballroom dancer

Carl Froch loves *Desperate Housewives*

Lewis Hamilton stood on Bill Clinton's foot

Amir Khan quit karate after losing to the opposite sex

Ledley King scared of rats

Greg Rutherford read all the Harry Potter books at least five times

Beth Tweddle has a fruit skin phobia

Serena Williams incredibly clumsy

Andy Murray addicted to Fantasy Football

Chris Ashton hates it when marks appear on his white trainers